LEADING CHRISTIANS TO MATURITY

John C. Blattner

Creation House
Altamonte Springs, Florida

Printed in the United States of America
International Standard Book Number: 0-88419-197-4
Library of Congress Number: 86-72774

Strang Communications Company
190 N. Westmonte Drive
Altamonte Springs, FL 32714

CONTENTS

Part IV
Wherever Eight or Ten Are Gathered...

Part V
Christian Community

Part VI
Putting It All Together: Four Case Studies

INTRODUCTION

Over the doorway of the volunteer fire department in a small Minnesota town is inscribed the slogan: "We'll Know Where We're Going When We Get There."

How often do Christian leaders feel that slogan applies to us!

Where are we headed with our pastoral care? At times it seems we give too broad an answer to the question, at times too narrow an answer.

Vision, in the broad sense, we have aplenty. We may say that our pastoral goal is "to win our generation to Christ" or "to build up the body of Christ" or "to serve the purposes of God in our day." These are all noble and scriptural goals. But they provide little concrete guidance on what we should be doing today, tomorrow, next week and next month.

On the other hand, our pastoral goals are often

formulated too much in terms of the specific tasks that make up our day-to-day life: planning and conducting worship services, preaching sermons, conducting visitation programs, and so on.

Again, all these are important activities that deserve to be done well. But they must be done in the context of a clearly thought-out understanding of what we are trying to accomplish. Otherwise we begin to feel like Alice, in *Through the Looking Glass*, who found she had to run as fast as she could just to stay in the same place. Vision, purpose and planning sink beneath the foam of day-to-day demands on time and energy. It is all too easy to be extremely busy but not very fruitful.

What we need is a workable pastoral strategy, one that ties together the many and varied activities in our job descriptions, and helps us keep them pointed toward our broader goals. Providing the outlines of such a pastoral strategy is the aim of this book.

The book draws its theme from that magnificent passage in which Paul summarizes the pastoral task: "Him we proclaim, warning every man and teaching every man in all wisdom, that we may present every man mature in Christ. For this I toil, striving with all the energy which he mightily inspires within me" (Col. 1:28-29).

To present every man mature in Christ—surely this must be the aim of our work as pastoral leaders in the church. But we must be careful not to let this scriptural charge become for us merely another of those over-broad goal statements that warms our hearts but fails to direct our steps. What is Christian maturity? What does it look like in our modern setting? How do we set about the task of leading our people into it? These are the questions we will try to answer.

In so doing, we will focus on maturity in Christian living rather than on Christian belief. Not that belief and its content are unimportant. They are, indeed, crucial. But so is the concrete, practical, day-in, day-out expression of that belief in people's lives. Our goal in this book is to correct the common tendency to focus on helping people believe as Christians at the expense of helping them live as Christians.

We will also focus on principles of pastoral care rather than on techniques. The aim is not simply to present a list of "ideas that work," but to try to understand the people we work with and the times we live in, so we can do a better job of applying the scriptural mandates for holy living to our actual situation.

The principles are derived not only from reflection on the Scriptures, but also from reflection on the actual experience of pastoral leaders who have put them into action and seen them bear fruit. At *Pastoral Renewal*, when we see a pastoral leader successfully helping his people grow to maturity, we have learned not merely to ask what he is doing that works so well, but also why it works so well. What can we learn from it that might be of help to other leaders in other situations?

Over the past ten years, we have had the chance to observe and learn from pastoral leaders working in a wide array of settings: new and growing churches, older and more established churches, covenant communities, prayer groups, renewal movements and other Christian organizations.

We have also learned from our own experience of building Christian community in The Sword of the

Spirit, an international and interdenominational community that features extensive development of lay pastoral care, integration of church-based and nonchurch structures, and experience both with rapid growth and with "settling in for the long haul." (Some of the case studies in Section VI describe branch communities of The Sword of the Spirit in which the contributors of this volume have labored.)

It is our conviction that the pastoral principles outlined here will be of help to those in all roles of Christian leadership. When we hear the words "pastoral work," we tend to think immediately of those who bear the particular title of "pastor." But in fact, many other Christians are also engaged in pastoral work in the broader sense: they participate in the process of leading Christians to maturity. Ministers and priests, elders of churches and communities, leaders of Christian organizations, prayer group leaders, seminarians, small group leaders, youth workers, campus ministry workers—all can profit from the principles outlined here.

It is also our conviction that the fundamental task of leading Christians to maturity is the same for all Christian pastoral leaders, regardless of their confessional background. This conviction is solidly borne out by our experience. Over the years we have seen these principles applied with equal fruitfulness among evangelicals, mainline Protestants, Pentecostals, participants in charismatic renewal, Roman Catholics and Orthodox. The challenges that all of us face in trying to live faithfully and fruitfully for Christ, in the midst of an increasingly hostile secular culture, highlight the common ground on which we can stand together, even as we acknowledge the important differences that divide us.

The book begins with an examination of where we all begin—the cultural context in which our people live, in response to which our attitudes must be formed, our understandings sharpened, our pastoral principles and methods developed and refined.

Next, it looks at the goal toward which our efforts are aimed, by discussing, in pastoral terms, some key elements of normal Christian living.

Then it discusses some important vehicles by which we can lead people from where they are now to where the Lord wants them to be.

Finally, it offers a look at some churches and communities that have applied the principles, to help us see what they look like "in the flesh."

The essays in this volume, while written by different people at different times, come together to form the outlines of a comprehensive pastoral approach. This approach underlies the total ministry of the Center for Pastoral Renewal and its monthly journal, *Pastoral Renewal*. It is our conviction that this approach can be of great value to all pastoral leaders trying to serve the Lord by leading their brothers and sisters into maturity in Christ. It is our prayer that it prove to be so for you.

J.C.B.

PART I

THE CONTEXT OF CHRISTIAN LEADERSHIP

The challenge of pastoral care is to help God's people live God's way of life in the midst of a culture that does not acknowledge God's sovereignty. The essays in this section analyze that culture, the effects it has on the people in our churches, communities and groups, and its implications for our service.

CHAPTER ONE

Wisdom in a Time of Change

by Peter S. Williamson

The last few decades have been difficult for Christian churches in the West. Most of the major church bodies have steadily lost ground during this period, judging by the usual standards of measurement. Even a cursory look reveals that Christianity's influence is waning, both in the personal lives of churchgoers and in our culture as a whole. Despite exceptions to this trend, it is clear that the Christian churches are in trouble.

Behind the difficulties lie two major changes in society, changes that have been taking place for some time: the de-Christianization of Western culture and the rapid social transformation resulting from modern technological development.

Culture and Technology

Not long ago Christians could count on society's laws, beliefs, and values to support the basic moral and even the doctrinal teaching of the Christian churches. To a large degree, society as a whole helped people remain faithful to Christianity, and church institutions helped them grow. Today's congregational and parish structures, as well as current approaches to pastoral care, took shape in a social environment that in many ways was conducive to Christian life.

But the last century—especially the last three decades—has witnessed a pervasive secularization of society. In many areas of life the influence of churches on the lives of individuals has been replaced by the influence of mass media, government, business and science. Today the church exists in a social environment that does not reinforce Christian teaching and is sometimes hostile to it: Christians today face circumstances analogous to those faced by the church in the few centuries of its existence.

But the de-Christianization of society is not the only force affecting the Christian churches. Two centuries of ongoing technological revolution have produced deep-seated social changes, many of which undermined the stability of personal relationships. In a pattern radically different from traditional society, industrialization and universal public education separate parents and children during most of the day. People are compelled to move from one metropolitan area to another according to the demands of a nationwide job market. These kinds of changes have reduced the strength of personal relationships. Many other such social changes could be cited.

Impact on the Church

Because the church exists in society, this unraveling of the social fabric is bound to affect it. Partly because of these changes, church leaders today have a very difficult job. Consider the following kinds of difficulties they often have to handle.

• In our fast-paced society, it is hard to find people who are willing to commit themselves to perform the various necessary works of service in the local congregation. For many members, active participation in the church seems to be low on the list of priorities.

• Pastoral leaders, especially those serving in the larger churches, are often unable to maintain adequate personal relationships with church members. Consequently, people who come for counseling often bring problems that have progressed so far that the person trying to help them can be of little assistance. If they had come earlier, the pastoral counselor could have been much more effective. Many other people never come for help, and their needs go unnoticed and unmet.

• Pastors have the task of advising many parents about how to handle wayward children. But usually the pastors are hard pressed to know what can be done to keep children in the church. Evangelical Protestant churches seem to be faring better than some of their mainline counterparts. But in competition with the powerful secular youth subculture, even they have a hard time keeping the children Christians.

• Church management, maintenance of schools, and various other aspects of church life keep ministers and priests busy, leaving them little time to take stock of what is happening with the people in their congregations or to try new pastoral approaches.

Clergy and lay people engaged in pastoral work experience these problems to varying degrees. The lot of pastoral leaders is by no means entirely bleak.

But problems like these are common, and Christian leaders need pastoral vision and wisdom to handle the difficulties that confront them.

Challenges of Renewal

Amid these difficulties, many Christians today are hopeful about the growth of various churches, organizations and movements that stress spiritual renewal as the fundamental solution to the church's needs. Among these are the steadily growing evangelical church bodies and organizations, the charismatic renewal in the Protestant and Catholic churches, and a variety of other movements that emphasize personal conversion and relationship with God.

But spiritual renewal does not cause pastoral difficulties to evaporate. On the contrary, church history suggests that spiritual renewal creates new and greater needs for pastoral care. Spiritual renewal brings people out of religious indifference to a point of wanting to be taught, counseled and directed in how to grow in the Christian life.

Movements of spiritual renewal usually also generate new groupings in which those involved in the renewal movement come together to sustain and grow in their new life in Christ. These new pastoral structures may range from prayer groups to communities to new denominations. They need appropriate leadership.

The increased demand for pastoral care that attends spiritual renewal usually calls forth lay involvement in pastoral work. Lay people in such movements are sometimes uniquely positioned to serve the other participants because of the similarity of their lives to those they are caring for. Lay people may do pastoral work on only a limited scale, confining themselves to personal counseling or the planning of programs. Or they may take more extensive responsibility for the lives of other

Christians. In any case, they need to be trained.

In addition to the needs that all pastoral leaders face, leaders of renewal movements and groups often must struggle with additional questions, such as, What kind of new structures will best serve what God is doing in the group? How should the individuals or group experiencing renewal relate to existing church structures? How should new leaders be selected and trained? How should new people be brought into the group and helped to grow as Christians? How can so many new people be cared for effectively? Again, wisdom is essential.

False Self-Confidence

For leaders of churches and groups in renewal, the road is not easy. They can easily make serious pastoral mistakes, often because of a false self-confidence. Knowing how much has seemed to happen spontaneously in their group by the sovereign work of the Holy Spirit, they may reason that planning for or guiding their group is unnecessary. Other pastoral leaders discover and apply a certain part of Christian truth and see it bear good fruit in people's lives. Assuming that this understanding of Christianity and pastoral care is complete, they stop learning, and their pastoral vision remains partial and inadequate.

Rapid increase in the size of a church or group may give Christian leaders an illusion of success and cause them to overlook serious inadequacies in what they are doing. The pastor of one charismatic renewal church told of a vague dissatisfaction that beset him, even after membership in his church had tripled within two years because of his vigorous evangelism and follow-up program. Because of his lingering uneasiness, he set aside a week for prayer and evaluation. During that time he felt the Lord showed him what was wrong: "You are not growing; you are just getting fat. You just have more people of the same kind." The pastor realized that though his church was growing in size, it was failing to bring anyone to Christian maturity and failing to mature as a Christian body.

When spiritual renewal movements thrust clergy and lay people into new pastoral roles, much is demanded of them. The issues they face are as difficult and serious as those faced by pastors of ordinary congregations.

What Is Wisdom?

The ability to care for others and bring them to maturity in the Christian life can be understood best in light of the scriptural teaching on wisdom.

The Bible presents wisdom as an ideal of life to be earnestly sought. "Happy is the man who finds wisdom, and the man who gets understanding, for the gain from it is better than gain from silver or its profit better than gold" (Prov. 3:13-14).

In the Old Testament, wisdom means a practical understanding that comes from God about living or doing something. Not an academic or theoretical understanding, it is a useful knowledge of the inner workings of something. The Hebrew word for wisdom, *chokmah*, often means simply the skill of a craftsman (Ex. 31:3,6). The wisdom given in Proverbs and the rest of the wisdom literature is concerned mainly with the skill of successful living: how to handle personal relationships with spouse, children and friends; how to use money; how and when to speak; how to relate to God. It is the special need of all in positions of authority (Deut. 1:13,15); God was pleased to make Solomon wise (1 Kings 3:10-12). Wisdom is attributed above all to God, who knows the inner workings of all creation.

The New Testament use of the term wisdom is largely the same as the Old Testament, with two notable modifications. The Greek word for wisdom, *sophia*, brought with it the connotation of philosophical knowledge (see 1 Cor. 1-2). Second, wisdom is sometimes used in the New Testament to refer to the whole of God's thoughts and plan regarding redemption (see Eph. 1:9). But it is clear from other passages (Col. 4:5 and Jas. 3:17, for example) that the early church continued to value wisdom in the traditional, Old Testament sense of the word.

Rightly Related

Scripture teaches that we acquire wisdom first of all by being rightly related to God: "The fear of the Lord is the beginning of wisdom, and knowledge of the Holy One is insight" (Prov. 9:10). The Lord is the one who imparts wisdom to those who, like Solomon, ask for it. The ability to speak words of wisdom is one of the gifts of the Spirit (1 Cor. 12:8). Paul writes that those who possess the Spirit have access to the very thoughts of God. Proverbs recommends various steps to gaining wisdom: studying and keeping the law, learning under the instruction of one's elders and other wise men and women, receiving correction willingly, and growing older—presumably learning from one's experience.

Clearly, the wisdom about living which most of the proverbs are concerned with is one of the most important needs of a pastoral leader. And, more specifically, Christian leaders today need to grow in *pastoral* wisdom, a practical understanding of how to build up the body of Christ, how to care for the lives of Christians. To meet the challenges of the church today, our understanding must increase.

Acquiring Wisdom

I would like to suggest four ways to acquire wisdom about caring for Christians and Christian groups.

1. *Pray for it.* "If any of you lacks wisdom, let him ask God, who gives to all men generously and without reproaching, and it will be given him. But let him ask in faith" (Jas. 1:5-6).

True wisdom comes by the revelation and inspiration of the Holy Spirit. Sometimes this can come as a sudden insight into a knotty pastoral problem, right after praying for wisdom. More often, however, God teaches us wisdom as we think about things. This is not a less spiritual process; it is the normal way in which God intends to form and use our minds. If we pray expectantly for wisdom and keep our minds attentive to the Spirit, we will find ourselves learning things in many different circumstances.

2. *Learn from the Scriptures.* Scripture prescribes some things about church life, and these we must simply accept in our pastoring as wisdom given by God. Being faithful to the gospel, celebrating the Lord's Supper or having elders who exercise pastoral leadership—these have to be part of our pastoral approach because they are part of the nature of the church as Scripture presents it. Scriptures also forbid certain possible pastoral approaches. Selling leadership positions in the church, for example, can be dismissed out of hand, since the Scriptures clearly see that as wrong. Our pastoral approaches, however wise they may seem to us, must not contradict the Scriptures.

However, the Scriptures can teach us more than the mere requirements and limits of pastoral practice. We can learn from models in the Scriptures without being bound to imitate them exactly. For instance, Jesus' method of training disciples can greatly help our understanding of how to form not only leaders but all Christians. Though it is not necessary to conclude that Jesus' approach to discipleship is the exact way Christian formation always ought to be done, we will want to pay serious attention to how the Lord did it.

Meditating on the Scriptures in the light of our pastoral experience, and meditating on our pastoral experience in the light of the Scriptures, can produce a deeper understanding of the scriptural principles of church life.

Insights From Others

3. *Learn from proven leaders and groups.* The Scriptures recommend listening to the instruction of wise men as one of the principal ways of acquiring wisdom (Prov. 13:14,20). If a man wants to become a carpenter, the best way is to find someone who is already skilled as a carpenter and learn from him. The same is true for pastoral workers.

We can discern which leaders and which Christian groups have wisdom (by "groups" I am referring to parishes and congregations as well as other Christian fellowships and organizations) by looking at the fruits of their lives and apostolic work. Many voices are clamoring to advise us today. Although they are saying very different things, they may all sound quite reasonable to us. We should make a point to learn from those who have been able to get Christianity to work successfully in their own lives and to help others live it too. Making visits to successful Christian groups and reading their literature can be instructive.

We should learn not only from those who have

wisdom today, but also from those who gained it in the past. Catholics and Orthodox believe that some aspects of church tradition establish a permanent pattern for church life. But all Christians, whatever theological weight they give to Christian tradition, can learn a great deal from the pastoral practice of Christians in the past. Of course, one needs to understand their historical context and use discernment in applying their experience. But works such as *The Rule of St. Benedict* and *The Journal of John Wesley* can teach us a great deal about caring for Christian groups. (For those interested in these particular books, Benedict's rule is available in a translation by A.C. Meisel and M.L. del Mastro from Doubleday-Image Books, and Wesley's journal in an edition by P.L. Parker from Moody Press.) Often, Christian pastors writing at a different time could see things that we are blind to because of our own cultural background.

Humility and openness are necessary if we are to learn from others, especially from Christians who are very different from ourselves. But basic pastoral concerns are essentially the same among Christians of even the most diverse theological and ecclesiastical backgrounds. Much can be learned from the people we suspect have the least to offer us. Catholics and Orthodox could learn from many Protestants about evangelizing, bringing people to a personal conversion to the Lord. For their part, Protestants could benefit from studying how Catholic tradition has allowed new groups and movements to arise within the Catholic Church while preserving the unity of the whole body.

It is important to distinguish doctrines from pastoral approaches. We can be faithful to the doctrines of our churches while being flexible regarding pastoral methods. We all have a tendency to canonize the way we have been doing something as the only right or scriptural approach. One pastor chided fellow pastors on this score at a recent conference. "I stand before you," he said, "a man who has discovered the genuine pattern of the New Testament church—29 times!" When we cling to our own way as the only way, learning something new obviously becomes difficult.

But Does It Work?

4. *Learn from ordinary human experience; pay attention to what works.* Of the four ways of acquiring wisdom, this deserves special attention, since it is the most neglected. In most things, people rely heavily on practical experience. But in pastoral care, the benefits of paying attention to what works are often overlooked. Our theories can be an obstacle. A pastor's belief that Sunday school or parochial school *ought* to be the chief means of evangelizing children and forming them as Christians may prevent him from seeing when these means are not doing so. Though God may at times want us to do something that to all outward appearances is not working, more often He wants to guide us by the fruitfulness of our labor. We should regularly evaluate what we are doing in terms of its results.

Many of the proverbs found in the Scriptures teach a wisdom that is not particularly religious but is just common sense. Some of it, scholars tell us, was borrowed from the wisdom literature of ancient Egypt and Edom. Exodus records that Moses would have been in real trouble without the friendly advice of the priest of the Midianites, who recommended he reorganize the people of Israel. Many of us who are pastoral workers today could profit from some commonsense thinking about how to use their time and how to organize the groups or communities which they lead.

Our ordinary observations about life, people and human relationships can be the Lord's means of teaching us. Other human sources of wisdom such as psychology and sociology can help us if we approach them with discernment. For instance, sociological studies about the effects of social environments on beliefs and values can help us see the need for Christian social environments. Such studies can provide us with insights about what kinds of social groupings most effectively provide people with support for their personal growth.

Human wisdom by itself is inadequate, but when it is subordinate to God's wisdom and put at God's service, it can be of real value.

Skillful Servants

To acquire wisdom through any of these four ways requires dedication. We need an inquiring mind on pastoral subjects. We must consciously decide to consider alternative ways something can be done, to investigate how other groups handle similar problems, and to reflect on our pastoral experience regularly, evaluating what we have been doing. Being part of a group of leaders who want to grow in wisdom together and who discuss their pastoral work can help a great deal.

God is at work in the churches, giving them strength to meet changes and challenges in society and to be His instrument in the world today. The leaders of the churches need to open themselves to learning more than they already know about pastoral service. Society is continuing to change, and ways of doing pastoral work which used to succeed no longer do, or soon will not. The Lord wants His servants to become more than skillful in the service He has given them. Paul has defined our task: "We are fellow workers for God. According to the commission of God given me, like a skilled master builder I laid a foundation, and another man is building upon it. Let each man take care how he builds upon it" (1 Cor. 3:9-10).

CHAPTER TWO

What Do We Expect?

by Kevin Perrotta

Shifts in expectations occur less perceptibly than changes in beliefs. Our expectations change as we are exposed to new things, become familiar with them, develop a tolerant attitude toward them, resolve to make the best of them, learn to take account of them in our planning and routine. One day we look back and compare our present attitude to our attitude several years before, and we recognize that we have undergone a subtle but revolutionary alteration in our thinking.

An instance of this is the matter of divorce and remarriage. In the last 15 to 20 years, many Christian leaders who never expected to see much divorce and remarriage among their people—I am thinking particularly of conservative Protestants and Roman Catholics—have, simply, come to expect it.

This is not to say that they have come to accept it, to think that divorce and remarriage are good or desirable. The great majority of these pastoral leaders continue to view divorce and remarriage as contrary to God's intentions. But while their beliefs have not explicitly changed a great deal, their expectations have.

This process has been going on with Christian leaders regarding other issues as well. Some, though not all, cluster around sexuality. For example, pastoral leaders increasingly expect that many of the younger single people in their care will enter degrees of physical intimacy with each other that the preceding generation of Christians would regard as totally inappropriate. This was brought home to me a while ago when I was speaking with one pastor about how he helps young Christians handle dating and courtship. His first remark was, "You have to teach a lot about forgiveness."

Expectations and Standards

The problem is not simply that pastoral leaders are no longer surprised when the Christians they are leading are unfaithful to the Christian way in major areas of life. The problem is that our altered expectations lead to changes in our pastoral practice.

This happens on a small scale when a congregation ceases to consider the divorce of members a subject for scrutiny by the church's leadership and adopts a merely affirming and supportive stance toward the couple.

It also happens on a large scale. For example, in the Roman Catholic Church, Cardinal Pericle Felice, speaking for the pope, in 1980 sharply criticized the methods of some Catholic marriage annulment tribunals. An annulment is a declaration that in the eyes of the Catholic Church the two persons were never married because they failed to meet one of the necessary conditions—for example, one of the partners was already married to a living spouse. In recent years, many Roman Catholic marriages have been annulled on the grounds that one of the partners was too psychologically immature to contract a valid marriage. This has prompted the criticism that some annulments look like a divorce—which Catholic Church teaching does not recognize.

In both cases, one goes on saying that divorce is against God's will, but acts in ways that imply that the official view is unrealistic.

Fornication offers similar examples. Some Roman Catholic theologians now advance justifications for sexual relations between engaged couples. Among even conservative Protestants, approaches have begun to be published which accept increasing physical intimacy between unmarried people, from petting to oral intercourse, as two people grow closer emotionally.

Here we see theory accommodating itself to practice while trying not to abandon (or trying to avoid *seeming* to abandon) the original Christian positions. The standard of behavior expected goes through a process of reconsideration and emerges as less than a clear rule of right and wrong.

Sometimes the definition is fudged. For instance, there is this line of reasoning: "Scripture forbids fornication. Fornication means only vaginal intercourse between unmarried people. Thus Scripture says nothing about whether single couples can engage in any other sexual practice. So petting in the nude and oral intercourse are acceptable."

Sometimes the standard is remade into an ideal. People are expected to move toward the ideal, but there are times when it is permissible to set it aside. Some current views of divorce and remarriage work this way.

In one way or another, the standard is, in effect, relaxed. The conscious or unconscious assumption is that the standard is unrealistic for everyone where they are now.

This was articulated by a speaker at a workshop on how to help people deal with anger. "We can't expect people to be like Jesus," he said. "Jesus was both God and a human being. We are just human beings." The man cited the situation of a woman in his church who was married to an alcoholic. How could she handle her anger as righteously as Jesus?

That is a good question, and in one sense the man's answer to it is correct. Only Jesus is perfect. We are redeemed sinners who have not yet been perfected by the Lord. So pastoral leaders cannot expect themselves, or anyone else, to be like Jesus in the sense of being perfect.

But the speaker meant more than that. He meant that it was unrealistic to teach people to handle anger—or any other aspect of life—as Jesus did, because we cannot do what Jesus did. He was God and man, and we are only men or women.

What is wrong with this way of thinking is that the Lord *clearly does intend* us to become like Him. "Follow Me." What else does that mean? What else does it mean to live according to the Spirit rather than the flesh in order to bear the fruit of the Spirit?

I suspect that, if pressed, the speaker would deny that he was trying to rewrite Scripture. He would say that all he was trying to do was be realistic: "Yes, Jesus calls us to be like Him. But in fact very many Christians are far from being able to do it." For example, this woman is the only Christian in her family and does not have close friends in the church. Her unhappy childhood has ill-prepared her to deal well with a disordered family situation. She lacks the spiritual resources to do more than react as an ordinary, well-intentioned, wronged human being.

Despite its seeming realism, this approach is fatal to pastoral work. Little by little the substance of the Christian life is worn away. Its Christ-like features are flattened by the pressures of a non-Christian world. The salt loses its savor. The pastoral leader no longer expects the men and women in his care to be leading full Christian lives.

Supportive Relationships

Thus what follows from a decline in pastoral leaders' expectations is often an erosion in the leaders' pastoral practice regarding basic standards of Christian living. What is it that precedes this decline in expectations? Or, more precisely, if pastoral leaders have come to expect Christian men and women to be having less success than in the past in living out important aspects of Christian teaching, what are the sources of the difficulties?

One factor that comes immediately to mind is the breakdown of Judeo-Christian values in society at large. But an equally important and less often noted factor is the weakening of the personal supports for Christian living in people's daily lives. The fabric of many people's personal relationships, such as family, neighborhood and church, has been unraveling. Consequently, Christians become highly susceptible to secular influences.

The view that a reinforcing network of personal relationships is important for Christian living is supported by a comparison of our current situation with that of

Christians in the past (or today outside the West). In periods when the level of mutual support within the church is high, Christians are able to maintain a high degree of faithfulness to scriptural teaching despite external pressures. Their leaders do not generally experience the temptation to change Christian teaching.

The early Christian centuries, for instance, were not filled with disputes over accommodating fornication or being sufficiently flexible regarding divorce and remarriage. The key reason is not that the Roman empire was a more hospitable place than the modern West for obeying apostolic teaching. The reasons were that Christians then effectively supported one another and experienced the power of the Holy Spirit.

Today, many of the patterns of modern society weaken these supports. Take, for example, the education of young people. As children progress from one grade to another, their time and interests are increasingly absorbed by secular educational environments—classes, extracurricular activities, athletics, peers. Involvement in home and church decreases. The process reaches its ultimate stage at the university level. Universities are large collections of independent individuals. Thousands of young men and women leave behind familiar formative and guiding relationships for weeks or months at a time. As a result they are quite susceptible to the influences of new ideas and ways of looking at life. In this sense the university stands as a paradigm of the atomization that is going on throughout contemporary society.

Practical Help

What conclusions can we draw from this line of thinking? I believe two are of particular importance.

First, in the long run it is futile to try to maintain Christian teaching simply by preaching it, defending it and fighting for it. In our rapidly changing social situation we must combat the pressures to reinterpret Christian teaching not only by arguing against the reinterpretations but also by finding more effective ways of helping people follow the teaching.

Much of the current erosion of faithfulness to historic standards of Christian behavior is a misguided attempt to deal with the fact that many people are having a great deal of difficulty living up to the basic Christian standards—or even perceiving them as being meaningful. It is not enough for us to demonstrate that these alterations are, in the final analysis, unrealistic because they are inconsistent with revealed teaching. If we want to see the churches fully restored to faithfulness in pastoral teaching and practice, we must develop ways of helping people meet the challenges they encounter to Christian living today.

Basic Strategies

A second implication of our reflections on pastoral expectations is that changes in Christians' behavior—to which we may be adjusting our expectations—are not necessarily due to shortcomings in our preaching, administration or carrying out of the duties assigned us. Certainly none of us is performing our duties perfectly. But people's problems are likely coming from a level more fundamental than our pastoral practices are reaching. The weakening of natural relationships in our fast-changing, mobile society is exposing the Christians in our care to secular currents and pressures.

If we want to apply remedies that will be fundamentally effective, we will have to do more than sharpen our skills and improve our programs. We will have to work at a very basic level. For a start, to deal with contemporary society's massive challenges to Christian living, every Christian needs a vital relationship with God that brings a personal knowledge of God's love and power and motivates him or her to make important changes in order to put God and His kingdom first. Where this kind of relationship is lacking, pastoral leaders must make evangelism of the baptized a high priority.

Further, Christians' relationships need strengthening. Christian social environments are needed as a counterweight to the secular environments of work, education and the media in which we must live. This means Christian leaders must enter some unfamiliar territory. For example, not only preaching is needed, but also practical teaching which shows people how to live out the New Testament instruction about relationships with other people.

The shift from a program-oriented pastoral approach to an environment-building approach is an even more challenging step. It means leading Christians into linking their lives together in love, commitment and service in everyday ways that support family life, stewardship of money and time, Christian sexual behavior, and the rest. It means developing a pastoral style that most Christian leaders today have not been trained for.

Have we been lowering our expectations for how well the men and women we lead are actually going to follow basic Christian teaching? If so, we should guard against the tendency to conform our teaching and practice to this shift. Of course we must deal with people where they are, but as someone has said, we are not supposed to leave them there, if where they are is trespassing important boundary lines laid down by God.

But in addition to maintaining clear teaching regarding the Christian way of life, we should examine the structures of people's lives to find the causes of the problems. Then we should consider what redirection of our efforts would get at those root causes.

CHAPTER THREE

Pastoral Priorities for a Secular Age

by Stephen B. Clark

At the beginning of 1812, Napoleon ruled most of Europe. He had defeated all the armies that had opposed him. He had provoked the resignation of the last Holy Roman Emperor, and had then married his daughter. He held the pope captive. He had everything he wanted, except for three details: Britain, Spain and Russia. In that year he decided to invade Russia.

Napoleon gathered an army, marched into Russia and trounced the Russians in a couple of major battles. The tsar's army made a last stand before Moscow but suffered a major defeat. By October 1812 Napoleon sat in Moscow surrounded by an undefeated army, the most powerful man the world had seen for a very long time.

Then a fire broke out in Moscow. No one knows how the fire started, although most think a Russian deliberately set it. The fire burned much of the city. By the time it was out, the army's food supplies and winter quarters were gone. Napoleon was forced to abandon the city. Heading west through the Russian winter with the tsar's troops at his heels, Napoleon's grand army disintegrated. Within two months of his greatest victory, his army, the most powerful in Europe, had virtually ceased to exist. Napoleon struggled on for two more years, but after Moscow he was a defeated man. The reason was not a loss on a battlefield, but the fact that he had been unable to keep his army alive.

There is a moral here for us. My title is "Pastoral Priorities in a Secular Age." The "pastoral" comes from the Latin word for "shepherd"—a person who cares for the sheep. The very simplest way to describe the care a shepherd gives sheep is to say that he keeps them alive. This is also the simplest way of saying what a pastoral leader does for people: he cares for them so that they stay alive as Christians. If they do not stay alive as Christians, there is nothing they can accomplish. It is very basic.

Many of us in Christian leadership are intent on affecting society with Christian values. If we are to do this, we must first pay attention to pastoral priorities. How will our efforts at social influence do any good if, while we are trying to affect society, Christians themselves are losing their Christian life? How can we have a Christian impact on society if we are unable to keep the people of God alive as Christians?

A few years ago Roman Catholics in the United States were pleased about the growing Catholic vote and the number of Catholics winning political positions. The assumption was that this would mean that Catholics' understanding of social justice would be better represented in government. How ironic, then, a couple of years ago, to see the cardinal archbishop of New York having his discussions with the Catholic governor of New York and a Catholic candidate for vice president who did not quite line up with the Roman Catholic position on abortion. It is fine to have Christians in political positions—if they take Christian stands and act in a Christian way. But if they have been "evangelized" by the secular culture, their presence will not matter very much. They will be no different from anybody else.

Defining the Goal

"Keeping Christians alive": what does this pastoral goal mean? First and foremost, it means helping men and women to be alive spiritually, to have spiritual life, divine life. They need to be united with God in Christ, living the life of grace.

The goal also means helping people follow the Christian way of life day by day. A Christian cannot live any way he chooses. Paul wrote to the church in Corinth: "Do you not know that the unrighteous will not inherit the kingdom of God? Do not be deceived; neither the immoral, nor idolators, nor adulterers, nor homosexuals, nor thieves, nor the greedy, nor drunkards, nor revilers, nor robbers will inherit the kingdom of God. And such were some of you. But you were washed, you were sanctified, you were justified in the name of Jesus Christ and in the Spirit of our God" (1 Cor. 6:9-11). Paul saw an intrinsic connection between the way Christians live and their eligibility to inherit the kingdom of God. He identified observable kinds of behavior as indicators of whether people were alive in Christ: how were they living, what were they doing, what were they avoiding?

Finally, "keeping Christians alive" means seeing that

they are able to pass on the Christian way of life to their children from generation to generation.

If we do not keep the Christian people alive in these ways, then all our efforts at evangelistic outreach and social influence will be buildings without foundations. If Christians do not have spiritual life, do not follow the Christian way of life day by day, and do not succeed at handing on that way of life to their children, then the Christian people will be like Napoleon's grand army, no matter how vigorous and successful some of our efforts may be.

Sing Our Way of Life

My assignment is to examine pastoral priorities in a secular age. I would say "in an *increasingly* secular age." I have previously observed that a lot of good Christian things are happening in the United States: we see a growth of interest in Christianity, a small growth in Sunday morning attendance, vitality of varying degrees in the more theologically conservative Christian groups. But, as I have noted, the statistics clearly show that here is a serious decline in people's living the Christian way of life. In regard to acquiring and using material wealth, in regard to sexuality and family life (fornication, divorce, abortion and the rest), and in many other ways, Christians are increasingly indistinguishable in the secular culture they live in. Less and less are they living that way of life which is integral to what they are as Christians. [See my article "Christian Advance or Retreat: Sorting the Indicators in American Society" in the preceding volume of this series: Peter S. Williamson and Kevin Perrotta, editors, *Christianity in Conflict* (Ann Arbor, Michigan: Servant Books, 1986).]

In that light, what should our pastoral priorities be? What is most important for us to do to help the Christian people stay alive as Christians in the midst of an increasingly secular culture? I would propose six priorities. The first three I will merely mention, in order to keep the right perspective before us. I will comment on the latter three at greater length.

Three Familiar Projects

The first priority is bringing people, including those who are Christians in little more than name, to full and complete conversion to the Lord Jesus Christ.

The second priority is spiritual renewal, that is, leading people into a lively, worshipful relationship with God, into a spiritual experience of Him, into the life and power of the Spirit.

The third priority is giving people teaching that grounds them in historic Christian belief and protects them from the unsound ideas flowing out in the world and through the churches as well.

Every pastoral leader needs to see that these needs are met in the people he is caring for, if they are to have and maintain life as Christians.

Less Familiar Dynamics

The other priorities have to do with what we might call "underlying dynamics."

The value of identifying underlying dynamics was illustrated by an attempt I made a couple of years ago at landscaping. I have had a *little* experience in gardening. My father made me weed, mow the lawn, and so on. So I thought I knew something about transplanting. Several shrubs had to be moved from one side of the yard to another; I dug new holes for them, carried them over, put dirt on them, and gave them a little water.

A friend of mine, whose father is a nurseryman and who actually knows something about transplanting, took a look at my effort and told me, "They aren't going to live." He offered to help. I noticed that he did things that it never occurred to me to do. He waited until the proper time to transplant the shrubs. Then he did something with the roots to prepare them. He fertilized them. After he transplanted them, he doused them with water day after day. Needless to say, my friend's transplants are doing fine, while mine have turned to orange skeletons. I did the obvious things, but my transplants did not live. My friend was successful because he understood the underlying dynamics of maintaining life.

Those of us with pastoral responsibilities often do not see underlying dynamics. We fail to notice what is undermining the Christian life of people in our care. In recent years, for instance, many of us have watched middle-aged couples in our churches and communities who have raised their children and seem to be happy enough suddenly get divorced. Why? we wonder. In the past, such couples would not have gotten divorced. They went so long; their marriage looked OK. Something must have been going on that did not appear on the surface. If we had been able to spot it, we might have helped them, and they might still be married. Now they have become part of the divorce statistics, and it is too late to do anything.

Let us look at three underlying dynamics of Christian living and the pastoral priorities that they lead to.

Environments

The first dynamic is the influence of social environments. An environment is simply a group of people who are together in some way. To use sociological terms, an environment is a stable social situation. In the Acts of the Apostles we are told of the church in Jerusalem that "all who believed were together" and "the company of those who believed were of one heart and soul" (2:44; 4:32). One of the reasons the early Christians stayed alive as Christians was that they were together, one in heart and soul, mind and spirit. They formed a Christian environment.

Consider the effects of a non-Christian social environment today—the university. We might think of virtually any university, secular or even religious.

What happens when Christian students come to the university? For the most part, although not in the case of every individual, in terms of Christian sexual morality, they will become less faithful. From the point of view of politics, they will become more liberal. In their views on social roles, they will become more feminist. Their preferences in clothing and recreation will tend to reflect current fashions on campuses across the country.

Why does this happen? Is it because of the courses the students take? Their courses are a factor, but not the chief factor. The changes happen to students who study mathematics as well as to those who study psychology. The changes in outlook occur mainly through the young people's interaction with an environment where certain values, attitudes and behavior are accepted. The consequences of their being in such an environment are generally predictable. They tend to absorb what is accepted.

We can all verify this dynamic from our own experience. We have all been in environments—a school, a job, a platoon, a club—in which we have begun to notice that we are getting changed.

"These Are My People"

Sociologists have discovered that we tend to adopt the values, attitudes and behavior of a social environment *to the degree to which we identify with it*. We are open to being affected by a group to the extent that we say, "I am one of these people. This is my group. I belong here."

This is an important insight. By and large, most people who consider themselves Christians do not belong to Christian churches or groups that function as social environments for them. Or, if their church or group does function as an environment for them, they identify with it solely for religious purposes. They do not say, "This is my group. These are the kind of people I want to be." Rather they say, "For religious activities I identify with these people." But for the values and attitudes that shape their lives, they identify with other groups of people.

It was not always this way for Christians in the United States. For instance, the urban Catholic immigrant parishes and the rural Southern Baptist congregations of the past were social environments with which members strongly identified and which, therefore, had a powerful influence on their whole lives. But as ethnic, regional and other loyalties have weakened especially since World War II, Protestant and Catholic churches have lost their place as the focus of Americans' social identification. Most local church bodies function largely as service centers offering specialized religious activities and assistance rather than as centers of their members' networks of relationships and way of life. Fewer Christians have Christian social environments with which they strongly identify. Consequently, they are strongly affected by the increasingly secular social environments in which they live, study, work and recreate.

If pastoral leaders are to help their people stay alive as Christians, one of their highest priorities should thus be to create an effective Christian environment for them. They should bring Christians together in such a way that they identify with one another: "I belong to this group. These Christians are my people. I want to be like them." This kind of Christian social environment needs to be strengthened where it is weak and restored where it has been lost.

Consistency

The second underlying dynamic has to do with the effect of patterns of social behavior on basic morality. Certain ways of doing things help us to be moral, while other ways of doing things make it difficult to be moral.

Christians generally see the importance of keeping the Ten Commandments. They know that there are some things that they absolutely cannot do: murder, commit adultery, steal. But they do not see the connection between social customs and keeping the commandments. As a result they adopt social patterns that are not conducive to being moral. They do not realize that there needs to be a *consistency* between their fundamental moral principles and the way they live. Because they are not concerned to be consistent, they get to a point where it becomes virtually impossible for them to remain faithful to basic moral precepts. They do not know where to draw the line, and so they get themselves into hot water.

Let us take the example of the sexual revolution. In its post-1960 phase, Americans' sexual attitudes and behavior have changed drastically. The studies indicate that sexual morality has been eroding for everybody, Christians included. Research shows that young Christians, even junior-high children from intact, churchgoing families, are joining the sexual revolution.

One reason for widespread sexual immorality among Christians is that pastors, single people, and parents accept social patterns that are inconsistent with Christian morality. They do not start the battle for sexual morality soon enough. By the time they get to the place where they make a stand for basic morality, they have already conceded so much ground that it is too late.

A hundred years ago Christians of every description would have been in complete agreement that sexual morality requires certain social customs. For example, Christians would have been united in the view that unmarried men and women should not spend much time together unless they are in a family setting or are explicitly moving toward getting married. Christians would have regarded it as common sense that single men and women should not spend time together unless they are chaperoned. And they would have agreed that single men and women should not touch one another sexually.

Christians of a century ago would have said that these social patterns were necessary in order to keep the Ten Commandments. Therefore they would have said these patterns were a part of sexual morality. A single man and woman spending time unchaperoned alone, for example, would not have been seen as committing the most serious kind of wrongdoing, but their behavior would have been considered wrong because of its inconsistency with living a chaste life. It was crystal clear to Christians of the last century that if young, single people are allowed to spend a lot of time together, are not supervised and are allowed to do all sorts of things in the way of touching one another, sooner or later they are going to "go all the way," as it is sometimes termed. Social survey statistics tell us that is exactly what happens nowadays.

The lesson is that if we draw up our battle line at the last possible point, we are likely to lose the war. We have to start much further back. We need consistency between our social patterns and our moral principles.

The same point applies to every area of morality. For example, we recognize spouses' permanent moral responsibility for one another and parents' moral responsibility to raise their children in the Christian faith. But if we also accept the self-seeking patterns of life that go along with materialistic acquisition in our increasingly secular society, then we will find that marriages disintegrate and children are not given adequate discipline and care. We will also find that Christians are having a difficult time keeping the commandments against lying and stealing.

Thus one of our pastoral priorities should be to see that in the various areas of their lives Christians are consistent, not just trying to avoid behavior that is most clearly forbidden, but keeping away from the social patterns that lead to it and are, in fact, shaped by un-Christian values. Our pastoral concern has to be not only to create Christian environments, but also to form in those environments a way of life that is consistent with essential moral principles.

Carriers

Finally, there are the underlying dynamics of what we might call "carriers" of anti-Christian values and attitudes. The term refers to contagious diseases. Some diseases can be caught by touching things that carry the infection. If we handle them, we start getting sick. This is often predictable. If we want to stay healthy, we need to stay away from such carriers.

When I began to do pastoral work, a couple of men who had been involved in homosexual activities came to me for help. They wanted to make a break with their homosexual activities. I did not know exactly what to do, and I did some reading on the subject and listened to some talks on tape. In one of the talks the speaker made a valuable point. He said, "Whatever you do, impress upon such people that they cannot go back to their gay friends. If they do, they will resume their gay way of life." He even gave a predictable period of time—several weeks—by the end of which a person struggling against homosexual practice who returned to the gay world would succumb again.

I told these two then that particular truth. One listened and, during the time I continued to have contact with him, he was able to reorient his life. The other ignored this advice, went back to his gay friends, and within the time period mentioned by the speaker he was back into homosexual activities. He made contact with the carrier that eroded the Christian commitment and way of life, and fell victim to the disease.

I suggest the following list of the most important carriers of anti-Christian values and attitudes today. It is impossible here to give each the attention it deserves, but it may be helpful at least to present them.

1. *Friends and acquaintances.* Who are your friends? Whom do you hang around with? These are the people who affect you.

2. *Models and authorities that a person accepts.* If

a football player who lives an immoral life is your son's great hero, odds are that he is going to have an affect on him. If your authority is a college professor with anti-Christian views, or you think Dr. So-and So is one of the world's greatest experts on child-rearing, even though his advice does not square with a Christian approach, you will be affected by them.

3. *Entertainment.* The time we spend in entertainment is not just off-hours. Movies and music that glorify immorality can spread infection most quickly.

4. *The mass media.* Television and recordings are crucial.

5. *Education.* What is taught in the courses? What is given in the programs?

6. *Work settings,* especially those with training that is designed to teach us how to do things and impart certain kinds of values to us.

Given the power of these carriers and given the anti-Christian views of life that they often carry in our increasingly secular society, it should be a pastoral priority for us to examine them closely. We need to open our eyes to how people in our care are using these carriers and how they are being affected by them. We need to help our people understand what is going on and teach them to avoid some things, control some things, counteract some things. This seems crucial in our current cultural situation.

A Disguised Blessing

I would say that if we neglect these three dynamics—environments, consistency and carriers—if we do not have a pastoral approach for dealing with these things, then the Christian way of life will tend to disappear among the people we are leading, unless there are some special circumstances. This is not, however, a reason for losing hope.

Some years ago I was living in an old house in which water began to seep into the basement. We were distressed at this and called in a workman to correct the problem. After a couple of days he came upstairs and said, "You know, you're lucky you had water in the basement." This was puzzling. Why were we lucky to have water in the basement? The reason, he explained, was that in order to find the source of the problem he had to uncover the foundations, which were not usually exposed to view. When he did this he discovered that the mortar between the stones was crumbling. Where a hundred years ago there had been hard mortar, there was not a gravelly material. This had caused the water problem. But if the water problem had not occurred, we would not have known that the foundations themselves were disintegrating. "If you don't do something about it now," the workman told us, "pretty soon there will be no mortar between your stones, you won't have a foundation, and you won't have a house." So we were blessed to have water coming in the basement. It gave us a chance to save the house.

As we look around and notice "water" coming in among the Christian people—secular values and behavior—we might account it a blessing. Perhaps the Lord is telling us that we need to look more carefully at the foundations and see if all the mortar is there that was there a hundred years ago. If not, we need to seek His guidance and help to begin to remedy the situation.

Part II

NORMAL CHRISTIAN LIVING

One of the basic principles of problem-solving is to ask the question, What will this problem look like when it is solved? If we do not keep the goal in view, it is impossible to move toward it effectively.

In this section we examine some foundational elements of normal Christian living, trying to answer the question, What does Christian maturity look like? The goal is not to provide an exhaustive or definitive answer, but to identify some key landmarks to guide us in our pastoral work.

CHAPTER FOUR

Radical Commitment to Christ

by Peter S. Williamson

The heart of being a Christian is a relationship with Jesus Christ. He is the one mediator between God and man. He makes it possible for us to enter into the presence of God. Through Him our sins are forgiven and we receive God's life. In Him the human race finds a new beginning.

The way that God has provided for us to enter a relationship with Himself is to turn to Christ and commit ourselves to Him. Commitment to Christ, consisting of faith and obedience, is the essential mark of a Christian. This commitment is focused and expressed in baptism, which all Christians see as important, although various traditions understand it differently. (Because my concern in this essay is the pastoring of those old enough to believe and obey, and because the views of Christians are so diverse on the matter, I will not attempt to relate what I say here to infant baptism.)

Our faith must rest in the gospel that Jesus announced as well as in God Himself. It is necessary to believe in Jesus' death and resurrection for the forgiveness of our sins, to believe that Jesus is both Lord and Christ and that He is coming again to judge the living and the dead. More than simply doctrinal assent, ours must be a personal reliance on God and on Christ as our savior and redeemer.

Our obedience to the Lord begins with repentance for the wrongdoing we have committed. Repentance is characterized by sorrow for what we have done, a renunciation of the wrong behavior, and resolve to go on and do God's will where we had previously failed to do it. It is expressed by prayer, asking God's pardon in the name of Jesus.

Faith and Obedience

But to be a Christian means more than turning to God at a particular moment; it means a life of faith and obedience. Jesus and His apostles expected believers to be *disciples*, to order every aspect of their lives by the commandments of God and the teaching of Christ.

Believers were called to place their relationships and their use of time and money under Christ's lordship. This involved a choice against those elements in the Christian's life and culture that were at odds with Christ's teaching. Neither family nor country, wealth nor pleasure, ambition nor friendship, was to take precedence over a Christian's relationship with his God.

From the moment of receiving new life in Christ the Christian was expected to take up a life of love of Christ and subordination and service to Him. As the apostle Paul says, "And he died for all, that those who live might live no longer for themselves but for him who for their sake died and was raised" (1 Cor. 5:15).

In the early church, when persecution was overt, it was easier to see who really had made a commitment to Christ. Also, in the apostolic age, most of those who entered the church made an adult choice to become disciples. Today in the West, Christians do not usually face physical persecution, and many enter the church by growing up in it, sometimes without making an explicit personal choice. Partly as a result of these changes, the church of the West today includes large numbers of people who lack a commitment to Christ who are weakly committed.

These people can be divided into four categories. Each kind needs a different sort of help in order to be brought to normal Christian faith and obedience to our Lord.

Cultural Christians

Cultural Christians are those who have grown up in the church or in a mostly Christian environment, and who more or less "go along." These Christians vary widely in their beliefs and behavior. The best believe in Christ, try to keep the Ten Commandments, go to church at least some of the time and pray occasionally, but their lives are not centered around serving Christ. The least committed cultural Christians profess belief in Christ and in the obligation to lead a moral life, but may not do so themselves. It is common for cultural Christians to view Christianity largely in terms of what they must do and what sins they need to avoid, if they want to go to heaven.

In the past, especially in societies that were predominantly Christian, the church has included large numbers of Christians like this. An inclusive approach to church life has even been a conscious strategy, with the hope of leading members of the church gradually to a deeper level of commitment to Christ. This essay is not the place to evaluate this strategy. Suffice it to say that as our society becomes increasingly de-Christianized, it becomes necessary for all to make an explicit personal commitment to Christ.

Cultural Christians need to be evangelized. They need to hear someone present clearly what God has done in Christ—the salvation, forgiveness and new life God is offering—and to be invited to respond personally. They need to understand that God is not distant, but someone who loves us, wants us to be in a personal relationship with Him, wants to give us fullness of life in Christ. Further, they need to understand that their relationship with Christ is not meant simply to be an aspect of their lives, but to be at the center. They need to renounce whatever in their lives is inconsistent with God's law and put their lives at the service of Christ and others.

Often the best way for a cultural Christian to grasp the Christian message is by seeing the difference between the kind of Christianity he or she is living and that of someone (or, better yet, a group of people) who is spiritually alive and genuinely committed to Christ. Some cultural Christians have a latent Christian idealism (perhaps currently directed toward secular ends). They can often be brought to see that loving God and our neighbor as Christ's disciples is the highest ideal. To this teaching must be added an understanding of the critical role of the grace of God, so that their understanding of Christianity does not amount to merely human idealism.

Cheap-Grace Christians

The second kind of Christians whose commitment to

Christ is subnormal is what I would call *cheap-grace Christians.* Like cultural Christians, they have heard part of the truth, but not all of it.

Some of these people have been told that all they need to do is believe that Jesus has freed them from their sins and personally accept Him as their savior, and they are Christians. What they have not been told or not told clearly enough is that they must repent of their sins to be forgiven and afterwards obey Christ. I know some people like this who are so confident in the orthodoxy of their doctrines and the fact that they are saved that they make no effort to relate to others in Christian love.

Other cheap-grace Christians have been taught a distorted picture of God. They have come to understand Him so much as a God of mercy, love and forgiveness that they have lost sight of His holiness and justice. They have not been taught that God insists on some standards and laws (such as the Ten Commandments). They have been told that it does not matter too much what we do if our intentions are good, and that God is quick to pass over the wrongs we have done. They have lost the proper fear of the Lord, which is the beginning of wisdom.

Dietrich Bonhoeffer coined the phrase "cheap grace," and his description of it bears repeating.

"Cheap grace means the justification of sin without the justification of the sinner. Grace alone does everything, they say, and so everything can remain as it was before....Cheap grace is the grace we bestow on ourselves. Cheap grace is the preaching of forgiveness without requiring repentance, baptism without church discipline, communion without confession, absolution without personal confession. Cheap grace is grace without Jesus Christ, living and incarnate....

"Costly grace is the treasure hidden in the field; for the sake of it a man will gladly go and sell all that he has....Such grace is costly because it calls us to follow, and it is grace because it calls us to follow Jesus Christ. It is costly because it costs a man his life, and it is grace because it gives a man the only true life."

Some cheap-grace Christians are well-intentioned and simply need to be reinstructed and brought to a personal decision to submit their lives to God. They need to have Christ's teaching about living explained to them, as well as how to seek His will for the particular decisions in their lives.

However, it must be said that for others, cheap-grace Christianity is a choice, a religious preference, if you will. Because they are attached to a way of life that Christ would not approve of, it may be difficult to persuade them He is concerned about how they are living. These people need to confront the words of Jesus: "Not everyone who says to me, Lord, Lord, shall enter the kingdom of heaven, but he who does the will of my Father who is in heaven." They need to be told what it means in practice to obey Christ by repenting of serious wrongdoing—immorality, theft, lying, drunkenness, and other practices incompatible with inheriting the kingdom of God (1 Cor. 6 and elsewhere). They need to learn that the gospel must issue in a new way of life.

Secularist Christians

Third, there are what I call *secularist Christians*. Many Christians have been formed by a modern view of Christianity that robs it of its supernatural and eternal aspects and, consequently, of its understanding of sin and redemption. "The faith once delivered to the saints" is reduced to "being nice to people" or, since nature abhors a vacuum, is replaced by humanistic psychology, humanitarianism, political activism or whatever philosophy is in style. Secularist Christianity is often accompanied by moral teaching flawed by the second kind of cheap-grace mentality described above.

My experience is that the average secularized lay person has not become highly committed to another gospel hidden beneath the surface of the secularist message. Thus his inadequate understanding of Christianity does not present much of an obstacle to the gospel. The best strategy for this kind of person is to expose him to the real thing, especially to Christians who are experiencing the power of God in answers to prayer and lives that are transformed by the love of God. By comparison, secularist Christianity, with its good intentions and uncertain views, seems barren and empty.

Sooner or later the secularist teaching a person has absorbed will have to be countered. But if the person's heart has been transformed by the knowledge of God, it won't be difficult for him or her to see the inadequacy of a secularized view of Christ or his former relativistic assumptions.

The task of winning to a genuine faith those whose Christianity has been replaced by another, passionately held system of belief is much more difficult. Often the fundamental doctrines of the faith have been reinterpreted in political or philosophical terms. Christian terms have come to mean something quite different. It is hard to bring such people to understand that the ideology they have come to love, even though it may be very idealistic and ethical, is not Christianity. Often an individual has significant social motivations for continuing on his current course, having to do with the approval of his peers, the media, or society in general.

There is often a powerful spiritual component to the difficulty these folks have in returning to orthodox faith, a difficulty attributable to the quasi-religious character of some 20th-century ideologies and schools of psychology. In their case, the words of Jesus apply: "This kind can only be driven out by prayer and fasting." But these people can be converted by the power of the gospel. It helps them to have someone talk to them who understands the ideology they have adopted.

Backsliders

Finally, there are backsliders who were previously committed to Christ but, for one reason or another, have not continued to follow Him. The means that will help backsliders turn back to Christ vary. Some need encouragement that Christ will help them overcome the obstacles that turned them aside, and perhaps some practical help. For others, the key is assurance that God loves them and wants to forgive them for the wrong they have done, if they will turn to Him. Still others need to be warned of the consequences of not being in a right relationship with God and to be told that their way of life must change. Almost all require personal care to lead them back, and a way of getting reconnected with a body of Christians who are sincerely living out their commitment to Christ.

Making the Message Real

Though there are many people who clearly fall into one of these types, there are also many others who combine two or more of these approaches to Christianity. Cultural Christians especially can be found in the other groups. It is important to add that the category in which an individual is found is no sure guide to the attitude of his heart to God. In each category there are individuals who have a deep longing for God, as well as individuals who want nothing to do with a divine person who has something to say about their lives.

In every case we must present the gospel in a manner tailored to the individual's need. In every case the grace of God at work in the heart of the individual is key. I have not detailed it here, but fervent prayer makes all the difference in our efforts to lead men and women to commitment to Christ. We are engaged in a spiritual work and in a spiritual battle.

In order to counter the secular world view of our age, I have found that one of the most important elements in preaching the gospel is making the message real. By this I mean helping the person see how God is at work now in the lives of men and women, and therefore that Christianity is not a theory or ethical system.

Exposure to Christians who have a vital relationship with Christ is one way to do this, especially if they can tell how God has acted in their lives. Books that provide this are another way of accomplishing the same thing. Encouraging the individual to pray and ask God for the help he needs, whether it is spiritual, material or physical, can help. Often the Lord will take that opportunity to make Himself known. These experiences serve both to build faith and to awaken in the heart of a man or woman a desire for God.

Finally, it is a mistake to focus our attention on the person's intellectual understanding of the gospel, without giving due attention to how he or she is living. As a friend of mine once commented: "Again and again I find that the struggle most people encounter with the gospel message is not intellectual but moral. We Christians need to be a lot better at exposing the seemingly attractive ways of the world, the flesh and the devil for what they are—deceitful and corrupt."

Often what is at the bottom of a person's resistance to committing himself or herself to Christ is a way of life or a pattern of behavior that he or she is reluctant to let go. At the right time, directly addressing this issue can help. The truth such an individual needs to hear is that in dying to ourselves we really do find life in Christ, and that the life Christ offers is far better than anything He asks us to give up.

CHAPTER FIVE

The Power of the Holy Spirit

by Peter S. Williamson

The normal Christian life is not only a matter of our following the Lord Jesus Christ. It is also a matter of the Lord living and working in us through the Holy Spirit: "If a man loves me, he will keep my word, and my Father will love him, and we will come to him and make our home with him" (John 4:23). Through the Holy Spirit our lives are transformed, and we are enabled to live as disciples of Christ.

The Christians of the New Testament had a living experience of the Father, the risen Christ and the Spirit of God among them. To aid us in evaluating how our Christianity measures up next to the normal Christianity of the New Testament, let us examine five aspects of life in the Holy Spirit that the apostles and the New Testament authors considered normative. I have chosen to highlight elements of the Spirit's work that reveal the difference His presence makes.

Knowing God

First, *the Holy Spirit enables us to know God experientially*. The author of Hebrews indicates the experimental dimension of normal Christian life when he refers to "those who have once been enlightened, who have tasted the heavenly gift, and have become partakers of the goodness of the word of God and the powers of the age to come" (Heb. 6:4-5). The light of the Holy Spirit is in some sense to be seen, the power to be tasted. The author uses images of sensory experience to convey the reality of spiritual experience.

Many of us are justifiably cautious about an emphasis on experience. We know it is all too easy to slide into the ocean of subjectivity that pervades our culture. Nonetheless, Scripture and the testimony of Christians throughout history present us with a type of spiritual experience that calls for our attention, an experience rooted in the objective facts of redemption. We have become children of God, and the Spirit helps us to know it (see Rom. 8:15-16). Paul boldly stated how much our knowledge of God and of the truths about Him depend on the work of the Spirit in us:

"For what person knows a man's thoughts except the spirit of the man which is in him? So also no one comprehends the thoughts of God except the Spirit of God. Now we have received not the spirit of the world, but the Spirit which is from God, that we might understand the gifts bestowed on us by God....The spiritual man judges all things, but is himself to be judged by no one. For who has known the mind of the Lord so as to instruct him? But we have the mind of Christ" (1 Cor. 2:11-12,15-16).

Just as boldly, John writes, "The anointing which you

received from him abides in you, and you have no need that anyone should teach you, as his anointing teaches you about everything, and is true'' (1 John 2:27).

It is the Spirit that enables us to understand and draw life from Scripture.

The very word ''knowledge'' means more than mastery of information. ''To know,'' as Scripture uses the term, carries with it the sense of personal acquaintance and an understanding grounded in experience.

Help in Prayer

Second, *the Holy Spirit makes a discernible difference in ability to pray*. The apostle Paul writes, ''Likewise the Spirit helps us in our weakness; for we do not know how to pray as we ought, but the Spirit himself intercedes for us with sighs too deep for words. And he who searches the hearts of men knows what is the mind of the Spirit, because the Spirit intercedes for the saints according to the will of God'' (Rom. 8:26-27). So we are exhorted to ''pray in the Spirit'' (Eph. 6; Jude 20). We know from other passages in Acts and 1 Corinthians of one particular form of prayer in the Spirit that was common among the early Christians and was clearly Spirit-enabled: prayer in tongues.

The Spirit's help in prayer was not just an individual matter but something that had an effect on the worship and social life of Christians, transforming occasions that used to be devoted to drunken reveling into gatherings that issued in praise, thanksgiving and spiritual joy. ''And do not be filled with wine, for that is debauchery; but be filled with the Spirit, addressing one another in psalms and hymns and spiritual songs, singing and making melody to the Lord with all your heart'' (Eph. 5:18-19). The Holy Spirit inspires adoration and worship in a way that is manifest in a body of believers.

Guidance

Third, *the Spirit is active in leading and guiding us.* Here, as in other aspects of the work of the Spirit, we must be careful not to identify too easily what takes place in our churches with what the early church experienced. I am speaking here about more than providential protection or blessing on the fairly mundane decisions of a church or religious organization, and more than the guidance that the Spirit gives through the good counsel of gathered leaders who are "full of wisdom and the Holy Spirit." These forms of blessing and guidance are important and were an important aspect of the development of the church. But what I wish to highlight is the normativeness of a further kind of guidance.

The beginning of the New Covenant marked the restoration of prophecy, which had disappeared in Judaism (Acts 2:17,33; 20:23; 21:9-11; 1 Cor. 12:10; 14; 1 Thess. 5:20). As Justin Martyr told the Jew Trypho around the year 162, "From the fact that even to this day the gifts of prophecy exist among us Christians, you should realize that the gifts which had resided among your people have now been transferred to us."

From the many instances of guidance in Acts, I will cite just one to illustrate how concretely the Spirit's guidance affected the outreach of the church:

"And they went through the region of Phrygia and Galatia, having been forbidden by the Holy Spirit to speak the word in Asia. And when they had come opposite Mysia, they attempted to go into Bithynia, but the Spirit of Jesus did not allow them; so, passing by Mysia, they went down to Troas. And a vision appeared to Paul in the night: a man of Macedonia was standing beseeching him and saying, 'Come over to Macedonia and help us.' And when he had seen the vision, immediately we sought to go on into Macedonia, concluding that God had called us to preach the gospel to them'' (Acts 16:6-10). In this Spirit-led manner the first apostolic mission to Europe began.

Power to Preach

Fourth, *the Holy Spirit empowers us to preach the gospel and to build up the body of Christ.* Today we run the danger of simply declaring that every church or evangelistic work is, like its counterparts in the New Testament church, Spirit-empowered. But is this so?

Consider Paul's description of his labors in 2 Corinthians, or his words to the Galatians. Paul writes, ''Does he who supplies the Spirit in you and works miracles among you do so by works of the law, or by hearing with faith?'' (Gal. 3:5). How many of us could settle a theological disagreement in the church or Christian group we are caring for by appealing to the people's common experience of the manner in which God gave them the Holy Spirit and worked miracles among them?

The fact that the gospel was frequently, even ordinarily, attested to by Spirit-wrought signs and wonders is a commonplace in the New Testament (Mark 16:20; Acts 2:43; 3; 4:29-30; 5:12-16; 1 Cor. 2:4-5). Unfortunately, little description is given of the ordinary Spirit-empowered exercise of some of the other gifts, such as those of pastors, teachers, administrators, contributors, exhorters and the like. Suffice it to say that unlike many Christians today, when the apostles and the early Christians referred to the Holy Spirit and His work, they never seemed to be referring to an undetectable difference that distinguished religious activities from what was merely human. They knew the Spirit, and wherever He was present there was a recognizable power and effect.

Strength to Overcome Sin

Finally, *the Spirit enables us to overcome sin and to live as new men and women*. It was the Spirit who communicated to Christians of the New Testament the consequences of Jesus' victory over sin and death, empowering them to obey Christ, "that the just requirement of the law might be fulfilled in us, who walk not according to the flesh but according to the Spirit" (Rom. 8:4). This was a behavioral change in the habits of ordinary people. It did not come primarily as a result of new information about what was right—the law had been long extant—nor did it primarily come from a program of discipline and moral training. This change in habitual behavior and character came as a result of the presence of the Spirit. It was itself a manifestation of spiritual power.

The transformation required the free consent of men and women, but it was much more than an expression of their individual or collective willpower. Men and women characterized by works of the flesh—fornication, idolatry, strife, jealousy, anger, carousing—became people characterized by the fruit of the Spirit (love, joy, peace, patience, self-control, and so on). This change did not happen automatically or overnight, but it did happen wherever Christians were sincere about following Christ.

But Is It for Today?

How does life in the Holy Spirit, as the New Testament describes it, characterize our lives and the lives of the parish, congregation or group to which we belong?

There is a wide variance in the levels of discernible activity of the Holy Spirit among committed Christians today. Large numbers of believers with a deep commitment to Christ actually experience very little of the Holy Spirit's work, though we know He is present and working in ways that are not so readily apparent. This was my personal experience for many years.

On the other hand, some individual Christians, groups and churches manifest one or two of the signs of the Spirit's presence to a high degree, but other signs hardly at all.

The guiding principle seems to be that Christians' experience of the Holy Spirit's work depends on what they ask for and expect. Thus, some Christians manifest the power of the Spirit in miraculous gifts or mystical prayer, others in preaching and evangelism, and others in growth in Christian character.

If we reflect on the history of the church, we see particular times and places where the power of the Spirit has been evident in the lives of ordinary Christians in a way more closely resembling the experience of the early Christians. First, we see this at the edges to the church, on the frontiers where the gospel is being preached. This can probably be understood as the special working of God's power in connection with the spread of the gospel.

Second, we can observe times of spiritual renewal or revival when life in the Holy Spirit as I have described it is characteristic of whole sections of the church. Examples of such movements of spiritual renewal include the monastic movement of the fourth and fifth centuries, the Franciscan and Dominican movements of the 13th, the Great Awakenings in 17th- and 18th-century

America, the early days of Methodism in the 18th century, and the Welsh revival in the 19th and 20th centuries—to name only a few.

On the other hand, large portions of the Christian people throughout history seem never to have experienced this blessing. Is it possible that the experience of the Holy Spirit's activity which the New Testament assumes, and which I have called normal, is reserved by God to particular movements in the church's past or for a few "saints" among us?

I don't think so. I believe we can learn a great deal that will help contemporary Christians experience normal life in the Spirit from reflecting on the Pentecostal-charismatic revival of this century.

The Pentecostal-Charismatic Movement

This movement belongs with the other examples from church history mentioned earlier. It is a remarkable instance of spiritual renewal affecting millions of Christians of nearly every Christian tradition around the world. It has helped many of its participants (although by no means all) experience normal life in the Holy Spirit. In many parts of the world it comprises the most spiritually vital sector of the church today. The churches and groups associated with it, on the whole, are the fastest growing in the world, and have been for at least the last quarter-century.

To learn from the Pentecostal-charismatic movement does not mean that we must accept its theology (or theologies, since there are many understandings of what God is doing within this broad movement). Nor do we need to approve everything that is done in its name. Abuses have occurred, as have "spiritual" phenomena which we may discern to be merely human, or even spiritual counterfeits. Humans can bungle, and Satan can imitate the gifts and working of God. But that should not stop us from recognizing and profiting from the grace that God is making available to His people.

At the heart of initiation into the Pentecostal-charismatic renewal is prayer for the individual, accompanied by the laying on of hands by other Christians, asking God to "baptize the person in the Holy Spirit." Very often what is sought is the kind of normal life in the Holy Spirit that I have described above. When the individual experiences a change in his relationship to God, usually understood to be evidenced by praying in tongues, the person considers himself baptized in the Spirit and initiated into the movement.

Various difficulties confront the outsider who wishes to learn from the Pentecostal-charismatic movement. First, there is the theological problem of relating this step to an individual's prior commitment to Christ and baptism. Don't Christians who have Christ have the Spirit also, especially since Jesus speaks of being born of the Spirit as an essential (John 3)? Many Pentecostal-charismatic theologies resolve this difficulty by saying that Christians who do not experience charismatic gifts and guidance do not have the Holy Spirit, or asserting the normativeness of a "second blessing" after that of initially turning to Christ. Many Christians find both of these views difficult to square with the whole of New Testament teaching about the relationship of the Spirit and the believer, as well as with the beliefs and practices of most Christians throughout the centuries.

A second characteristic problem, common but by no means universal among those in the Pentecostal-charismatic movement, is to become focused on one aspect of normal life in the Holy Spirit—usually the gifts of the Spirit and in particular the gift of tongues—as the primary criterion for discerning whether or not an individual is filled with the Spirit. Now it is important for people to have an idea of whether or not they experience normal life in the Spirit, but there are problems with using the gift of tongues in this way. All aspects of life in the Spirit are important, but there may be a tendency to overlook some of them if the gift of tongues or spiritual experience is focused on. Moreover, it does not seem clear from the New Testament that the ability to pray in tongues was a gift God gave to all believers. Also, some of those who eventually receive this gift do not experience it immediately on being prayed with, but instead can point to other manifestations of the Spirit's presence with them.

A third common difficulty in the Pentecostal-charismatic movement is the tendency to confuse spiritual experience with emotional experience. One consequence is that those who are easily aroused emotionally consider themselves to be experiencing life in the Holy Spirit, and being emotional comes to be identified with being spiritual. The other side of the problem is that people whose emotional responses are somewhat weaker or less openly expressed wonder if the Spirit is really at work in them.

The fact is that experiencing a richer life of the Holy Spirit, especially for those who have been very desirous of tasting God's life more fully, can be an emotional experience, but it is not always so.

A Practical Approach

How can difficulties be overcome so that we can learn from the Pentecostal-charismatic movement? The interdenominational community I belong to, The Word of God, has been successful in helping ordinary believers enter into normal life in the Spirit through what we have learned from the Pentecostal-charismatic movement, while avoiding some of the problems.

We make it a practice to pray with everyone who wishes to join us for a full life in the Holy Spirit. We speak about the importance of being "baptized in the Holy Spirit," although we do not insist on that term with those who object to it. We do not say that Christians who have not been prayed over do not have the Spirit, nor do we teach the doctrine of a "second blessing." As an interdenominational community, we accept that different Christian traditions understand these realities differently.

We do teach that the Lord wants all Christians to experience the power of His Holy Spirit in their lives so that they can become the kind of people He wants them to be and accomplish what He wants them to in His service. When those who are already Christians are prayed with for a full life in the Spirit, most of us understand what is taking place as a release or personal appropriation of the power of the Spirit.

We do not look on the new experience of the Spirit's working as in itself any mark of spiritual attainment of maturity. On the contrary, we understand it as a work of the Holy Spirit given to help us become godly men and women. Appropriating the power of the Spirit belongs properly to the process of entering the Christian life.

Praying with people to enter more fully into the life in the Holy Spirit has made a difference for almost all the Christians we have prayed for, regardless of their previous Christian experience or maturity. How much of a change individuals experience varies. For some who do not have much personal experience of God's working, it is a big change. For others, who have long known the Lord and experienced His help over many years, it means perhaps a deepening of their ability to worship, an opening up to new spiritual gifts, or a new power to deal with an area of stubborn sin.

The basics of our approach to helping Christians appropriate the Spirit's power can be summarized in five principles:

1. *Make sure the foundation is firm by leading all to make or renew their commitment to Christ.* This entails presenting the gospel in a simple way and giving instruction in how to respond. We teach people as concretely as possible what it means to have faith (relying on God's Word) and to repent (turning away from sin and turning to God). We follow up this teaching with individual personal contact aimed at determining whether or not the person has taken these steps and, in particular, has set aside any serious wrongdoing of the kinds described in 1 Cor. 6:9-10 and elsewhere in Scripture.

2. *Explain what life in the Holy Spirit is meant to be like and how to enter into it.* The five or six elements of normal life in the Spirit mentioned at the beginning of this article can provide something of a guide to what needs to be communicated here. These elements are best described, not only in Scripture, but from the personal experience of those who are doing the instructing. Personal testimony that describes the difference the Holy Spirit makes in one's life makes concrete the meaning of life in the Spirit and builds faith that such a life

is really possible.

The way that people enter into a deeper life in the Holy Spirit is simply by asking God for it. He is the only One who can give us the Spirit, and He wants to do so:

"Ask, and it will be given you; seek, and you will find; knock, and it will opened to you....What father among you if his son asks for a fish will instead of a fish give him a serpent?....How much more will the heavenly Father give the Holy Spirit to those who seek him!" (Luke 11:9-13).

We have learned to encourage people to ask the Lord for the life of His Spirit and for spiritual gifts with expectant faith. They ought not to seek a particular experience, but a change in their relationship with God such that He is at work in them in a new way. Different people have different kinds of initial experiences of this new work of the Holy Spirit in their lives, and we found that initial experiences do matter in the long run. We ask for and receive this greater working of the Holy Spirit in faith, sometimes even thanking the Lord before we discern what God has done, as an expression of our confidence in Christ's words. Learning to ask God for things with expectant faith may be one of the greatest lessons the Pentecostal-charismatic movement has to teach the church.

3. *Do not shy away from spiritual gifts, but instead desire them and ask for them.* This is the instruction of the apostle Paul (1 Cor. 14:1; 1 Thess. 5:19-22), but some of the gifts are a scandal to many of us—on the far side of a cultural barrier. However, if we want normal life in the Holy Spirit, we will have to submit ourselves to the Spirit's unfamiliar ways.

We instruct those we are praying with to ask specifically for the ability to pray in tongues. We also suggest they ask for the other spiritual gifts, especially prophecy.

For those who are not personally familiar with the gift of tongues I should say that, contrary to the claims of some of both its advocates and detractors, it is not an ecstatic or necessarily emotion-charged form of prayer. Like all prayer, sometimes it is deeply felt and at other times it is not. We have learned to instruct people to pray for the gift of tongues because of the advantages it brings. Besides being helpful in a person's prayer life, it strengthens the faith of the individual in the presence of the Holy Spirit in him or her. Yielding to the gift of tongues helps the individual move beyond a naturalistic approach to the Christian life to a greater realization that we live a supernatural life. This is important in the rationalistic, scientific, secular age in which we live. Often, exercising the gift of tongues functions as a gateway to the exercise of some of the other gifts of the Spirit, especially those which are least like ordinary human abilities.

4. *Teach those who have entered into a deeper life in the Spirit how to grow in the Lord.* It is important that people understand at this point that the goal is Christian maturity, that they are just beginning and that they have much more to learn. Prayer, study of God's Word, Christian service and some degree of Christian community need to be part of their lives if the life of the Spirit is to increase and deepen within them.

The new people need to be instructed about handling trials of their faith that are sure to come and about resisting temptation. Those who are not very familiar with the Christian way of life need to be directed to solid teaching that will round out and complete what they have already learned.

5. *Lead them into Christian community.* God has made human beings interdependent in many respects, and this goes for spiritual matters in a particular way. The degree to which people continue to live normal life in the Holy Spirit is directly related to the degree to which the church, fellowship or small group they are part of is also living normal life in the Holy Spirit. Life in the Spirit is a matter of faith, and the faith of the Christians we share our lives with will tend to shape our own faith in God's working.

If we lead people into a deeper life in the Holy Spirit, we have a responsibility to help them enter some relationship with a group of Christians who will support them.

Never-Ending Renewal

With some regularity, all of us need to be renewed in our life in the Holy Spirit. The cares of this world and the weakness of our human nature can drag us down and undermine our faith. We can be tempted to live like ordinary men and women, not only by sinning but also by expecting no more help from God than the world does. When this happens, we need to turn back to Him, confess our faults, and ask His pardon and help.

The Lord wants us to experience the power of His Holy Spirit. He wants us to live a supernatural life in Him, and He will be quick to help us if we ask Him to increase and renew His life within us. This is something the Lord wants to do in us as a matter of course when we gather with other Christians to worship, to share in the Lord's Supper, to celebrate Easter, Pentecost and the other commemorations of the Lord's saving acts.

CHAPTER SIX

Fruitfulness in Service

by John Keating

"I'm frustrated and bored, and I don't know what to do."

I looked with surprise across the table at the young woman. She was attractive and capable, and I knew her to be a serious Christian. Yet I could see that something was amiss in her life.

"I'd like to be doing more with myself. But my church just doesn't offer any meaningful opportunities for someone in my position," she went on. "There are lots of activities I could get involved in, but they don't seem to have much point. I've been getting more concerned with myself lately, and way too invested in my career. I know I shouldn't be this way, but I don't know what to do about it."

My young friend was struggling with a problem that faces many Christians. For a variety of reasons, she was not making an adequate response to the presence of God in her life. As a result, she was finding her spiritual life dry and frustrating. She was spending less time with God in prayer and reading the Bible. Her thoughts, time and money were going more and more into self-centered interests. In the terms of one common New Testament image, her life was not "bearing much fruit."

To some, the young woman's lack of "fruit bearing" might seem of secondary importance. After all, she had clearly decided to follow Christ, she was a faithful church member, she avoided serious sin. But she was right to be troubled.

In the Scriptures the Lord emphasizes the importance He places on fruitfulness in His people. When God chooses a people for His own, speaks His Word to them, and pours out grace and blessing on them, He expects results. "I am the true vine, and my Father is the vinedresser....I chose you and appointed you that you should go and bear fruit and that your fruit should abide" (John 15:1-2,5,8,16).

The bearing of fruit is a sign of a healthy branch, the manifestation of the inner vitality it receives from the vine. For Christians, spiritual fruitfulness is the visible indication of God's life in the body of Christ and in its individual members. Far from being an optional extra, fruitfulness is an integral part of normal Christian living. Because it is by its fruit that a tree is known (Matt. 7:16-20), the absence of fruit, or the bearing of bad fruit, is disturbing evidence of something spiritually awry among the people of God.

Each Has a Part to Play

Christian fruitfulness has more than one dimension. Most fundamentally, Christians are called to bear in their own lives the fruit that manifests God's life within them.

This personal fruit-bearing begins with "the fruits that befit repentance" (Luke 3:8) and proceeds to "the fruits of righteousness" (Phil. 1:11; Heb. 12:11) and "the fruit of the Holy Spirit" (Gal. 5:22ff). This is the process of taking on the character of Christ, of "being changed into his likeness from one degree of glory to another" (2 Cor. 3:18).

Christians are also called to bear fruit in Christ's service. Jesus portrays the call to discipleship in these terms: His disciples are those appointed "to go and bear fruit" (John 15:16), fruit that is borne "in every good work" (Col. 1:10).

The Christians of the New Testament expected fruitful service to find expression in the lives of all the members. Theirs was not a church with a small number of highly active workers and a silent majority of Sunday pew-sitters. All were members of one body contributing to the "common good" (1 Cor. 12:7), employing their gifts "for one another, as good stewards of God's varied grace" (1 Pet. 4:10). This understanding of service for all according to the gift of God underlies Paul's teaching in Romans 12 and 1 Corinthians 12, and that of Peter in 1 Peter 4. Whether one's role is great or humble, prominent or unsung, each has his or her part to play.

The early Christians' service to God found expression along two lines: spreading the gospel and building up the Christian body. For the most part, spreading the gospel was not done by public preaching or random canvassing but by bringing God's Word to those close to home—family, friends and the rest.

Building up the body entailed services in which many members took part, some of which were done for those outside the body as well: almsgiving and works of mercy, including relieving the afflicted, caring for widows and orphans, helping in cases of urgent need (Rom. 12:8; 1 Cor. 8 and 9; 1 Tim. 5:10; 6:18; Titus 3:14; James 1:27); practicing hospitality (Heb. 13:1-2; 1 Peter 4:9); and the exercise of the various spiritual gifts (Acts 11:28; 21:8-9; Rom. 12:3-8; 1 Cor. 12:4-11, 27-31; Eph. 4:11-16; 1 Peter 4:10-11).

Converted to Servanthood

Effective service by all was woven into the fabric of the early church. How might contemporary Christians recover this normative aspect of Christian living?

If Christians are to be strong and effective in the service of God, they must begin with a personal conversion to the mentality and character of Christ (see Phil. 2:1-11). Put simply, they must not merely perform acts of service, they must *become servants*. Only in this way can they be like their master, the One who came "not to be served, but to serve" (Mark 10:45). Until such a conversion occurs in individual members and becomes the prevailing mentality of the church or fellowship, the capacity for Christian fruitfulness will be seriously limited.

Conversion to servanthood is of special importance in today's world. Many Christians, imbued wih selfish values, have oriented their lives toward personal fulfillment, and their relationship with Christ has a diminishing impact on them. Others carry their search for self-fulfillment into their spiritual lives. In some cases they become like spiritual sponges, absorbing inspiring teaching and experiences but not offering themselves for service. In other cases they may strive for service positions but with self-serving motives—the desire for recognition, honor, power or simply "feeling good about themselves."

True Christian servanthood, the prerequisite of fruitful service, is cut from an entirely different piece of cloth. It develops from the willingness to lose one's own life for the sake of Christ and His kingdom (Mark 8:34-38). It cannot remain a mere good intention but is to be palpably expressed in generous sacrifice of one's time, money, preferences and position (among other things) for the glory of God.

As pastoral leaders we can foster people's growth in Christ-like servanthood. Some principles have already been discussed in the preceding chapters on personal commitment to following Christ and receiving the power of the Holy Spirit. Here are some others.

The power of personal example. As valuable as teaching on Christian servanthood can be, words alone will not suffice. It is essential that the reality be embodied in the lives of those who are the pastoral leaders. We ourselves must demonstrate the character of Him who came "not to be served but to serve." The call to discipleship must be communicated by a disciple. The cost of following Christ should be explained by one who has counted and begun to pay the price. We cannot expect to lead out people further than we ourselves have gone.

Instruction. Many Christians today stand in need of a redirection of their aspirations, from secular goals to Christ's model of servanthood. This exchange can be fostered by instruction from the Scriptures which highlights the imitation of Christ (see Phil. 2:5-11 for an example of Paul's use of this method).

People also need to learn concretely what the character

of a servant is. Some of the essential traits of Christian servanthood are conspicuously lacking in modern life, and so Christians have not necessarily had the chance to learn what it means to be a servant. Pastoral leaders can address this need through instruction and illustration, especially from the Scriptures.

I have found that one of the biggest problems in churches and Christian groups is simply that when people are entrusted with responsibilities, they often drop the ball. Instructing people in being responsible, true to their word and faithful to their commitments can greatly enhance their fruitfulness in service. For others, instruction in Christian meekness and humility, in zeal, and in perseverance will pay dividends in their future service.

Many people do not know how to work with others or take directions. Preferring their own way and placing greatest confidence in their own judgment about how to serve, many people are unreceptive to instruction, slow to follow directions and unwilling to hear constructive correction. If they are to become profitable servants, it is crucial that they learn the value of being receptive to teaching, directions and correction. Teaching from the Scriptures, especially the wisdom literature, on the value of being instructed and corrected provides people with the grounding for this change of attitude (Prov. 9:7-9; 10:17; 12:1; 13:18; 15:12,22,31,32; 19:20,25; 21:11; 22:17-18; 23:12; 27:5-6; 28:23; 29:1).

Help with managing time and money. We can greatly assist people in becoming fruitful servants by helping them acquire mastery over their use of time and money. Then they are actually able to put their time and money at God's disposal. Again and again I have seen Christian students helped by some simple instruction in how to set priorities and how to schedule in light of those priorities. A little wisdom about disciplined use of time has enabled them to invest considerably in Christian service while maintaining and even improving the quality of their other involvements.

Helping people get a grip on their finances is similarly useful. Christians who have control of their money are better able to direct it into the Lord's service. One of the expressions of Christian fruitfulness is financial generosity (1 Tim. 6:18), both in almsgiving and in supporting the work of the Lord. For many Christians, financial giving constitutes a major outlet for service, one that should not be underestimated. While some people avoid more costly expressions of generosity or salve their troubled consciences by throwing money at good causes, it is also true that a large number of people who spend many of their waking hours working for a living have only a few hours per week available for service, and are able to make some of their most sacrificial contributions to the Lord's work through the giving of money.

It is also true that Christians with sincere intentions to serve the Lord can be tripped up by failure to handle money responsibly. This is a pastoral concern that we may need to give attention to as we are helping people grow in servanthood.

Training. Once Christians have embraced the ideal of Christian servanthood, they are ready for more specific training. Such training has two complementary components: instruction (usually in a course setting) and apprenticeship (personal instruction, supervision, and advice given by one experienced in the service to another who is learning it).

An all-too-common tendency is to offer only step one, and call it training. This, however, is often inadequate. Training begins with teaching but proceeds to working that teaching into the lives of those being trained until they can successfully do the task themselves. A football coach can give "chalk talks" until he is blue in the face, but unless he gets his team out on the field, going through drills, running plays and scrimmaging, his team will not be ready for the opening of the season.

Matching people with services. In many churches, taking on responsibilities of service is considered a mark of special generosity rather than a part of normal Christian living. Where this is the case there are usually too few people to do all things that need doing. Some volunteer and work very hard; others—including some of the more gifted—choose not to get involved. Those who do volunteer are usually welcomed into whatever role of service they would like to get into, because there often do not seem to be enough people to fill all the slots. As a result, it is difficult to assign people on the basis of where their gifts lie. The church ends up with some people working hard in areas where they are not the most spiritually gifted.

It is better when people undertake services on the basis of mutual discernment by person and pastoral leader on where God is gifting them. However, the key to being able to work this way is not merely more discernment. It is also necessary to have a larger number of people offering themselves for service—in fact, to have all the members of the church or fellowship actively entering into service. Then it is possible to make wiser choices about who should do what tasks.

Thus, if we want to move toward giving greater attention to how God has distributed gifts to people, we have to aim at a change of mentality in the congregation or group. We need to work toward a situation in which everyone considers it normal to be actively giving time and energy to Christian service and is committed to doing so.

CHAPTER SEVEN

A Distinctive Way of Life

by Kevin Perrotta

We are probably all familiar with the impression that the early Christians made on the inhabitants of the Roman empire: "See how they love one another." Retellings of Christian history less often describe how, for much of the first two centuries after Pentecost, the common view was that the Christians were "haters of the human race." In fact, both of these outsiders' impressions offer some insight into normal Christianity.

A quotation about Christians' care for one another comes from the late second century. The writer, Tertullian, who defends the Christians, explains that monthly, voluntary collections were taken up and the funds spent "not on banquets and drinking parties but to feed the poor and bury them, for boys and girls who lack property and parents, and then for slaves grown old and shipwrecked mariners, and for any who may be in the mines, on the penal islands, in prison." The emperor Julian, who tried to reverse the trend toward Christianity in the fourth century, asked his pagan priests, "Why do we not observe that it is in their benevolence to strangers, their care for the graves of the dead, and the apparent holiness of their lives that they have done most to increase atheism?" (by which he meant Christianity).

But earlier, when Christianity was brand new, it had a very negative public profile. When the Romans grew angry at Nero for burning the city in A.D. 64, he diverted their wrath toward the Christians, who were already unpopular. Persecutions during the first two centuries were often sparked by public outcry rather than government initiative.

Why this unpopularity? One historian writes that "the conviction that Christians were guilty of hatred for the human race" arose from their "apparent aloofness from the common life, so much so that Christians came to be called the "third race," neither pagan nor Jewish, but a race apart." The Christians kept their distance from the common entertainments, from the schools and hospitals (which had a pagan religious dimension), and from luxurious habits of dress, as well as from the communal religious practices. Christians were different—too different, in most people's view.

Whether non-Christians admired or despised them, everyone could see that the early Christians were a distinct people living a distinctive way of life. As people, for example, they had an evident care for one another. And they handled the aspects of daily living—family and work, time and money, ambition and anxiety—in a noticeably distinctive way.

Non-Christians who came into contact with Christians

in the Roman empire were, to a great degree, witnessing normal Christian living. The New Testament teaches that Christians are supposed to live as members of a people, following a God-given way of life.

Instructions for Daily Living

We usually think of the Christian message mainly as a set of beliefs, and miss the New Testament's emphasis on the body of teaching about the Christian way of life. Jesus made it a central part of His ministry to instruct His disciples in the life God intended men and women to live (for example, the Sermon on the Mount and the Last Supper discourse). The apostles and early church leaders made it a central part of their pastoral work to hand on and explain this instruction. Under the inspiration of the Holy Spirit the writers of the New Testament passed on this teaching to the church for all time. It forms the measuring rod for determining the soundness of Christians' lives. As Paul wrote to the Romans, "Thanks be to God that you who were once slaves of sin have become obedient from the heart to the *standard of teaching* to which you were committed" (6:17; see also 2 Tim. 1:13; 2:2).

At the core of this daily-life teaching is the understanding that Christ came to make it possible for men and women to become sharers in God's own nature (2 Peter 1:4), to become like Him (Matt. 5:48; 1 John 3:2). The early Christians saw the New Testament teaching about how to live as a continuation and perfection of the teaching given to God's people in the Old Covenant. Jesus' revelation made it possible to live more fully in accord with God's intentions.

In his book *Gospel and Law*, C.H. Dodd has noted that much of the New Testament follows a pattern:

sections giving instruction in the truths of salvation are followed by sections in which the practical consequences are spelled out. The epistles, for example, often begin with teaching about the work of Christ and conclude with directions about how to live as Christians; for instance, Romans, Galatians, Ephesians and 1 Peter. The *kerygma* ("proclamation" of the good news) and further instruction in the realities of the faith can be distinguished from passages presenting the *didache* (practical "teaching" about living—pronounced did' a kay).

Dodd identifies seven major propositions in the *didache*:

1. *The New Testament Christian is enjoined to reform his conduct.* For instance, Paul writes to the Ephesians: "Put off your old nature, which belongs to your former manner of life and is corrupt through deceitful lusts, and be renewed in the spirit of your minds, and put on the new nature, created after the likeness of God in true righteousness and holiness" (4:22-24; see also Rom. 12:1-2; 13:11-14).

2. *The typical virtues of the new way of life are set forth.* "But the fruit of the Spirit is love, joy, peace, patience, kindness, goodness, faithfulness, gentleness, self-control" (5:22-23; see also Col. 3:12).

3. *The proper Christian relationships within the family, the primary unit of the Christian community, are reviewed.* "Wives, be subject to your husbands, as to the Lord....Husbands, love your wives as Christ loved the church....Children, obey your parents in the Lord, for this is right" (Eph. 5:22,25; 6:1; see also Col. 3:18-21; 1 Peter 3:1-7).

4. *Right relationships within the Christian community*

are set forth. "Let love be genuine; hate what is evil, hold fast what is good; love one another with brotherly affection; outdo one another in showing honor" (Rom. 12:9-10; see also Col. 3:13-16; Phil. 2:1-4).

5. *A pattern of behavior toward pagan neighbors is described.* "Conduct yourselves wisely toward outsiders, making the most of the time. Let your speech always be gracious, seasoned with salt, so that you may know how you ought to answer everyone" (Col. 4:5-6; see also 1 Peter 2:12,18).

6. *Correct relationships with constituted authorities are defined.* "Be subject for the Lord's sake to every human institution, whether it be to the emperor as supreme or to governors as sent by him to punish those who do wrong and to praise those who do right" (1 Peter 2:13-14; see also Rom. 13:1-7).

7. *There is a call to watchfulness and responsibility.* "Be sober, be watchful. Your adversary the devil prowls around like a roaring lion seeking someone to devour" (1 Peter 5:8; see also Eph. 6:10-18).

Faithful to the Teaching

Christ, the apostles and the leaders of the early church considered the teaching about the Christian way of life to be the norm for Christians. They viewed the *didache* not as a distant ideal but as something that ordinary people would actually live out. Conversion meant new behavior: "By this it may be seen who are the children of the devil: whoever does not do what is right is not from God, nor he who does not love his brother" (1 John 3:10). "By their fruits you shall know them" (Matt. 7:20).

The early church was not perfect. But the early Christians followed the Christian way of life sufficiently well that their distinctiveness—along with their bold announcement of the gospel—brought on them almost three centuries of persecution in the Roman empire, and at the same time helped to attract thousands of men and women to Christ, even though commitment to Him could end in martyrdom.

In our own day it cannot be said that Christians in the West are following the teaching of Christ in a way that makes them particularly distinct. At a time when Western societies are swinging away from Christian values, Christians' lives are generally failing to become more clearly distinguishable. Rather, as society becomes less Christian, so do Christians' own patterns of life.

The picture that emerges from sociological studies is one of the persistence of certain key Christian beliefs, such as the divinity of Christ, but the erosion of Christian behavior. For example, specifically religious practices have been declining: Many people continue to believe in God, but fewer attend church on Sunday. Many continue to believe the Bible is God's Word, but far fewer read it regularly.

A survey by the Christian Advertising Forum in 1982 concluded: "There is a clear distinction between Christianity as a system of beliefs and values, and the manner in which people who profess to be Christians exercise those beliefs and values in their daily lives. The survey results suggest that scriptural exhortations to lead a Christ-like, Bible-based life-style are consistently ignored. American Christians have been captivated by secular opportunities and possessions."

A director of the United States Catholic bishops' office on family life once said that the increase of divorce and abortion among Catholics pointed to their abandonment, in practice, of Christian values. Another Catholic sociologist compared American Catholic families with their secular counterparts this way: "Their values may differ. But their behavior doesn't."

Evidence also suggests that many churchgoing young people are unfaithful to Christian standards regarding sexual behavior.

The causes of the current situation are complex, and so the solutions must come from several angles. Many Christians need to be led to a more explicit commitment to follow Christ and to a greater openness to the power of the Holy Spirit. In order to live out a distinct way of life, Christians need to be more committed to and supportive of one another in the body of Christ. New approaches to pastoral care are also needed.

But certainly one of the reasons for contemporary Christians' failure to live according to New Testament teaching is simply that Christian leaders are failing to present the teaching fully, clearly and with practical wisdom about how to apply it to modern circumstances. Some practical teaching does get communicated in the course of preaching, counseling, Bible studies, and so on within the local Christian body. Some also comes through Christian television programs, magazines and books. But few churches and fellowships offer a comprehensive curriculum aimed at passing on the New Testament *didache* about Christian character, relationships and the rest. People receive bits and pieces of Christian teaching in ways that are often contradictory and almost always incomplete.

Thus, a necessary element in leading Christian people back to general faithfulness to scriptural teaching must be a pastorally wise presentation of that teaching for our own day. For many Christian leaders, the starting point will be a recognition of pastoral responsibility in this area and a closer study of the biblical *didache*.

Making It Work

Christian leaders who seek to pass on the New Testament *didache* to the Christians in their care will face numerous challenges. In the social environments where we all live, varieties of a "secular *didache*" are being promoted. Television and the newspapers are filled with selfish solutions to life's problems. The schools are open channels for "value-free" propaganda about how to relate to adults, choose a career and handle sex. Workplaces are often dominated by gossip and slander and a "go for it, you deserve it" mentality. Nevertheless, a wise presentation of the New Testament teaching can have a powerful effect on Christians who are seeking to understand how to live out their faith. To pastoral leaders seeking to do this, the following advice may be offered:

1. *Integrate the didache in the total pastoral care in the local Christian body.* What I am proposing is that pastoral leaders give their people a comprehensive program of instruction, a curriculum, that faithfully explains the New Testament teaching about the Christian way of living. The New Testament teaching is itself the *standard* for Christian living. What we need to formulate is a *presentation* of it that helps people live up to the standard. Our presentation of the daily-life teaching is a pastoral tool which, along with other aspects of pastoral care, helps fellow Christians take on a new way of life.

If we want to help everyone in the church or fellowship live in accord with the New Testament standard, we will need to set up our curriculum in such a way that everyone is brought through it. We will also need to establish the instruction as a step of the process by which new people enter the Christian body we are leading.

As a central element of the life of the church, practical teaching about how to live is the responsibility of the overall leadership of the local church body. It is not a detachable responsibility that can be left to people who have a professional background in religious education or a talent for effective speaking. The main leadership must develop the presentation as a key element of the pastoral care by which they are leading the Christian body into a way of life pleasing to the Lord.

Communicating, as it does, the scriptural teaching about how to live, and coming from the leaders of the church body or Christian group, the presentation has real authority. It sets the standard for behavior and relationships in the church or fellowship. Thus when an issue arises about how to raise children, the body of practical teaching sets the ground rules for all the members. When a dispute arises among the members, there is a body of teaching which all members recognize as necessary to follow (the obligation to seek reconciliation, going to the other party directly, and so on).

The leaders not only present the instruction with the authority it has as a communication of God's Word. They also call the members to live it out day by day, offering both encouragement and correction. Of course, if the leaders are to call others effectively to live out the teaching, they must first of all recognize its authority over themselves. Their own obedient efforts to put the scriptural teaching about character and relationships into practice is crucial.

2. *Keep the didache rooted in the kerygma.* The practical teaching about living is possible in Christ by the power of the Holy Spirit. The daily-life teaching rests on the foundation of God's saving work in Christ and men's and women's response to Him.

Thus the first pastoral priority is to communicate the gospel effectively. It will do little good to provide better practical teaching to people who have not personally responded to the gospel or do not experience much of the presence of the Holy Spirit. The New Testament pastoral approach is to urge Christians to "live a life worthy of your call." If people have not personally responded to the call of Christ, our presentation of the *didache* can become an elaborate appeal to willpower, a lengthy exhortation to try harder, even a manipulation of feelings of guilt. Without personal commitment to Christ and the power of the Spirit, the motivation and the means to live out the practical teaching will be largely lacking. And unless Christians continue to be fed on the fundamental truths of the faith, they will find it increasingly difficult to live out the teaching.

In addition, we should keep the perspective that the *didache* is itself good news because it is God's wisdom for living in a way that works. Surely we have all had the experience of discovering that. I myself could not enumerate the ways that grasping a scriptural principle has made life more peaceful and work more successful.

3. *Present a program of practical instruction about living.* If our instruction in Christian character and relationships is to be helpful, it must be practical and concrete. Christians in our churches and groups need not only to hear that they must love one another, be faithful,

train their emotions, resist the devil, tame their tongue, and so on. They need to know what those directions actually mean. What do they like in real life? How does a person go about putting them into practice? If our presentation is vague and merely inspirational, it will fail in its main purpose. As pastoral leaders we need a clear enough understanding of the scriptural teaching that we can tell whether people are succeeding or failing in living it out. And the people we are teaching need to be able to tell, too.

Our presentation also needs to help people apply the New Testament teaching to their particular life situations. Another way to say this is that people need instruction about handling their roles and responsibilities according to God's intentions. Children need teaching about how to relate to parents and other adults. Young men and women need to be taught about the Christian way of settling on a direction in life and seeking a spouse. Husbands and wives need to learn how to serve one another and their children in their respective roles. Scripture provides principles and models in these areas which we need to grasp and communicate.

4. *Teach from Scripture, and look for developed presentations of the scriptural teaching.* Through the centuries Christians have used Scripture directly in teaching about how to live. While it is helpful to summarize and synthesize the scriptural *didache*, it remains the case that Scripture itself has a peculiar effectiveness for teaching. Traditionally, the wisdom books of the Old Testament have been widely used, and of course so has the practical teaching about qualities of character and principles of relationships given in the New Testament.

It is also wise to look for books and tape series in

which other Christian leaders have already thought through the questions about how to present the biblical teaching, and which offer pastorally wise advice about how to apply it.

Giving practical, scriptural instruction about the Christian way of life is a tool not only for helping individual men and women live more closely according to the pattern that God intends for human life. We should aim at more than helping fellow believers go out and do a better job following the Lord in all their separate circumstances. Christian living is not essentially individualistic but corporate. So we should also be working to build up Christians' life together. Much of the New Testament teaching about how to live has to do with being a people who have a common way of life: "Bear one another's burdens. Love one another with brotherly affection. Address one another in psalms, and hymns, and spiritual songs." It is to this corporate dimension of Christian living that we shall turn our attention next.

CHAPTER EIGHT

Brothers and Sisters in Christ

by Kevin Springer

At the Last Supper Jesus prayed to His Father that Christians might "be brought to complete unity, to let the world know that you sent me and have loved them even as you have loved me." While there may be speculation about the exact meaning of "unity" in Christ's words, this much we know for sure: non-Christians should be able to see the love of God in the way Christians relate to one another. Visible love and unity among believers is a part of normal Christian living.

Realizing this, the leaders of the church in the New Testament period formed highly committed groups in which Christ's command to love one another was lived out—communities where individuals grew to spiritual maturity and cooperated with each other in advancing God's purposes.

The early Christians did not see themselves as isolated individuals, only in a formal sense "members one of another.'' Their interdependence and love amazed pagans, helping to convert some of them to Christ. Indeed, the witness of Christians' love for one another in the first three centuries of the church was so powerful that many historians think it was a major cause of the spread of Christianity. The initial winning of converts, says John G. Gager in *Kingdom and Community*, ''cannot be regarded as the key to the continued growth of the Christian movement. There needed to be something further to retain the loyalty of converts through time. This something was the sense of community—open to all, insistent on absolute and exclusive loyalty, and concerned for every aspect of the believer's life.''

In strong communities Christians also found protection from the corroding influences of the non-Christian culture. The early Christians ''believed that they had been called to a higher quality of life than could be expected of their society,'' writes Abraham J. Mahlerbe in *Social Aspects of Early Christianity*, ''and they took measures to safeguard it through their communities.''

But we would be mistaken to think Christians formed committed communities only for the sake of evangelism or resistance to pagan culture. The basic reason for their unity was an understanding of the gospel—that in Christ God is raising up a new race of men and women, the people of God, joined together as a body. To the Romans Paul said, ''In Christ we who are many form one body, and each member belongs to all others'' (12:5; see also 1 Cor. 12:27).

The Goal: Life as a Body

Many pastoral leaders today narrow their goals to assisting changes in individuals: repentance, conversion, prayer and Scripture reading, growth in faith, avoiding wrongdoing. But God's norm is that individual Christians come to maturity as they enter and live in the body of Christ. We are called to "attain to the *unity* of the faith and of the knowledge of the Son of God," growing up "in every way into him who is the head, into Christ, from whom the whole body, joined and knit together by every joint with which it is supplied, when each part is working properly, makes bodily growth and upbuilds itself in love" (Eph. 4:13,15-16). A key mark of Christian maturity is the ability to live fully as a member of a body of Christians who love and serve each other, maintain peace and good order, and work together for the cause of Christ.

Scripture's view of the corporate nature of Christian living means directing our pastoral efforts not only at helping individuals but also at building up the body of believers. But while most of us would acknowledge this goal in principle, in practice many of us operate on the basis of a different model. We devote our energies to providing religious services rather than drawing fellow Christians into strong relationships with one another.

While in the typical parish or congregation there is a core of more committed people who may develop some degree of personal care and support for one another, most members experience the church mainly as a service institution where they go for various kinds of religious activities. In a Protestant setting the activities might be the preaching on Sunday, Bible study or a counseling program. In a Catholic or Orthodox setting people might come mostly for the liturgy and the sacraments. In both cases people may be receiving good teaching and experiencing God's grace, but their relationships with each other remain essentially unchanged. A real body of Christians is not formed.

In addition, even if the religious activities are good, they will not have their full effect in many people's lives if the people do not have strong Christian relationships. People need the example and help of older and wiser Christians in order to put Christian teaching to work in their lives. Listening to good preaching and receiving the sacraments can become divorced from leading a Christian life throughout the week if a person does not have support and help from other Christians.

By providing religious services without calling Christians into commitment to each other as brothers and sisters in Christ, the church accommodates itself to modern individualism. The individualist treats human relationships functionally and seeks to maximize his independence. In confrontation with this mentality, Christian leaders are called to assert the scriptural ideal of subordination to God and interdependence with Christian brothers and sisters.

Scripture provides a picture of normal Christian living. In the picture we can see principles of normal Christian body life. An examination of these elements can help guide our pastoral efforts.

Shared Life

In Acts, Christians are described as a group of people devoted to "the apostles' teaching, fellowship, to the breaking of bread, and prayer." They met every day. They ate together. They prayed together. They provided for each others' material needs (2:42,46).

The Greek word *koinonia* often translated "fellowship" in Acts 2:42 and other New Testament passages (for example, 1 John 1:3), means holding things in common, sharing. The shared life that Christians had with one another was an expression of their fellowship with God in Christ and in the Holy Spirit (see 1 Cor. 1:9; Phil. 2:1; 1 John 1:3).

In Jerusalem, Christians placed their lives in common. This is what made them a community. Further in Acts we read, "All the believers were one in heart and mind. No one claimed that any of his possessions was his own, but they shared everything they had" (4:32; see also 2:44-45). Members continued to maintain individual ownership while recognizing that others' needs had a claim on their resources (see 5:3-4). The Christians' approach to their material possessions was a concrete indication of how they were regarding the rest of their lives: not as their own, but at each other's service.

One measure of the depth of the shared life among the members of the early Christian communities is that they knew one another well enough to recognize who had the gifts and character to become leaders. The twelve told the members of the Jerusalem community to select men who were "of good reputation, filled with the Spirit and wisdom," to oversee the distribution to the widows (Acts 6:3). Paul instructed Timothy that to become a presiding elder a man should be "temperate, sensible, dignified, hospitable...gentle, not quarrelsome, and no lover of money. He must manage his own household well, keeping his children submissive and respectful" (1 Tim. 3:2,3-4). The criteria indicate that the early Christians knew each other not just in their participation in certain religious activities but also in a variety of daily-life situations—at home, at work, in friendships, observing how each other spent their time and money.

More evidence of the extent to which the early Christians had a life in common comes from the practical teaching about how to live as Christians which the New Testament authors gave to the members of the early churches. If the first Christians had not truly placed their lives together, how would they have been able to "rejoice with those who rejoice and be sad with those in sorrow" (Rom. 12:15)? Why would they need to be told to practice forbearance and think of what is best for each other (1 Thess. 5:15)? It is only to people whose lives are deeply shared that one says, "You must speak the truth to one another, since we are all parts of one another" (Eph. 4:25).

It was precisely because the Christians in Colossae had a life together that Paul instructed them as he did in Colossians 3:12-17. Often we consider the qualities that Paul mentions here, such as kindness and humility, to be individual characteristics that Christians ought to develop. They obviously are that. But we miss the full picture if we look at them only in an individualistic manner. Paul is describing qualities that should characterize their life together. He clearly intends that they should consciously shape this common life, telling them to speak with wisdom rather than with foolishness or gossip, to sing psalms rather than drinking songs, to be at peace with one another rather than allow jealousy and resentment to divide them.

Thus throughout the New Testament, instructions about how to live the Christian life *assume* that the early Christians had a life together. But to the extent that Christians today do not have a common life and come together mainly for religious activities, it is impossible for us to put much of this instruction fully into practice.

Because there is little common life in most churches today, there is little for the teaching to give shape to.

Having a real life in common necessarily meant sharing not only help, gifts and resources, but problems also. In the Christian communities of the New Testament, where shared life, knowledge of one another and mutual care were considered part of normal Christian living, members' personal weaknesses, temptations and sins could not remain exclusively private matters. People who meet often in each others' homes, share meals and have a practical concern for each others' material needs cannot at the same time regard personal privacy as an almost absolute value, as many Western Christians do today.

Rather, the New Testament portrays fellowships of Christians who encouraged and helped each other with the difficulties of living the Christian life—"bearing each others' burdens and so fulfilling the law of Christ" (Gal. 6:2). The members recognized the responsibility of the community's leaders for guiding and correcting them in their efforts to be faithful to the Christian way of life (see 1 Thess. 5:12-14; Heb. 13:17). This could only happen if the leaders knew the lives of their fellow Christians.

In a situation where people inevitably knew a lot about each other's faults and weaknesses, the early Christians saw the importance of avoiding slander, gossip and private judgments (see Matt. 7:1-5; 2 Cor. 12:20; 1 Tim. 5:13; James 4:11-12; 1 Peter 2:1). The New Testament clearly teaches that individuals' personal problems are not matters to be broadcast to the world. But at the same time, the New Testament authors do not suggest that individuals will deal with personal problems on their own, without the knowledge and support of the appropriate Christian brothers and sisters.

Before moving on to other aspects of the early Christians' relationship with one another, it is worth noting one hint the New Testament gives us about how the church leaders of the time facilitated a common life. It appears that one way they averted the rise of institutionalism in larger churches was by organizing subgroupings for shared life and pastoral care, such as the groupings of the church that met in various homes (Rom. 16:5,14,15; 1 Thess. 5:27; Col. 4:15).

Commitment to One Another

Christians in the New Testament communities saw themselves as a new creation in Christ (2 Cor. 5:17; Gal. 6:15), the new Adam (Rom. 5:14; 1 Cor. 15:45). They understood themselves as a new race of men and women (1 Peter 2:9). This produced a new relationship with one another. Old barriers were overcome. Jews and Gentiles, men and women, slaves and free men, all found themselves joined together in Christ.

This new relationship was expressed by the term "brethren"—brothers and sisters—which is the most common New Testament word for Christians. Time and time again the apostles exhorted Christians to love one another with brotherly love (1 Peter 1:22; Heb. 13:1; 1 John 3:17).

Being brothers and sisters was a concrete reality, not a sentimental notion. The meaning of "brethren" was viewed against the background of the relationship of brotherhood under the old covenant. The people of Israel were given a special responsibility for one another as members of one people. These responsibilities were spelled out in passages such as Deuteronomy 15 and

23 and Leviticus 19. To be brothers meant having a concrete duty to care for one another's material needs and to serve one another.

That this care for one another's material needs was seen as an essential element of Christian brotherhood is demonstrated by such passages as 1 John 3:16-18 and by the daily distribution to the needy in the Jerusalem church. It is also implied in Paul's instructions to Timothy about the care of widows and about families' responsibility to support their own members so that the church would not be burdened (1 Tim. 5:16; see also Heb. 13:3; James 1:27). The collection among the churches of Greece and Asia Minor for the Jerusalem church when it was enduring a famine shows that the responsibility of brotherly care extended not only to members of the church within the city but to other communities as well (1 Cor. 9; see also Gal. 2:10).

Our situation in Western countries contrasts sharply with the New Testament churches. Most church members' commitments to each other today are quite limited—to attend certain functions, to obey certain rules, to support certain activities.

Becoming a People

The Christians of the New Testament period saw themselves as a distinct people, the people of God (1 Peter 2:9-10). This meant that while they took part in the life of the society around them and sought its welfare, their primary identification was not with the empire they lived in or with their particular ethnic background, Jewish or Gentile, but with the Christian people.

To understand what Peter meant when he called the Christians a people, it is helpful to examine what is meant for the Jews of the time to be a people, because the early Christian communities sprang from the background of the synagogue life of the Jews. Peter explicitly draws a parallel between the Jewish and Christian communities by addressing his letter to the Christians of the "diaspora"—using the term for the communities of Jews outside Palestine. These Jewish communities formed distinct bodies within the larger Gentile cities. They lived under their own law, followed their own customs, were guided by their own authorities and had their own institutions of education and mutual aid.

The New Testament portrays Christians as a people, joined together in orderly communities, with a distinct way of life, under the guidance of pastoral leaders. The elders are explicitly spoken of as ruling or governing (1 Tim. 5:17). These elders have the authority to care for the lives of those in their charge and to correct the behavior of the members of the church if they are disorderly or seriously contrary to the Scriptures or apostolic teaching. The Christian communities had their own courts to settle disputes among members (1 Cor. 6:1-6).

While most of our churches and Christian groups are far from the model-community living that early Christians viewed as normal, many churches and groups do have some degree of shared life and mutual commitment. The challenge that most pastoral leaders face is not to build full community from scratch, but to raise the level of community where we are. This task will require wisdom, the power of the Holy Spirit, patience and much more.

Without going into detail, a few general pointers may be offered:

1. *Assess the current situation.* Which elements of

body life are we already experiencing? (Building on strengths is usually a sound approach.) Which missing elements would prevent us from moving forward?

2. *Ask the Lord's help and learn to follow His leadings.*

3. *Get help from Christians who have successfully established life as a body.*

4. *Provide members with a vision.* Awaken their hunger for a deeper level of community by teaching about some of the elements of the first Christians' life together.

5. *Begin with those who have the character and gifts to become leaders.*

6. *Increase the level of commitment gradually.* A way to begin is by drawing members into sharing about their relationship with God, spiritual life, and so on, then leading them to share with one another how other aspects of their lives are going. Next encourage members to serve one another in practical ways.

7. *Keep things clear* regarding what commitment is expected, who has made this commitment, and who the leaders are and what their authority is.

Part III

ONE-TO-ONE PASTORAL CARE

One of the most effective tools for leading Christians to maturity is one-to-one pastoral care: committed personal relationships in which pastoral leaders can tailor their efforts to the unique gifts and needs of particular individuals.

The essays in this section present the scriptural rationale for such ministry, outline its benefits and limitations, and offer practical advice for integrating it into the total pastoral effort.

CHAPTER NINE

What Did It Mean to Be a Disciple?

by Peter S. Williamson

Several years ago Billy Graham was asked, "If you were pastor of a large church in a principal city, what would be your plan of action?" Graham replied, "I would get a small group of eight or ten or twelve men around me who would meet a few hours a week...and pay the price. Over a period of years I would share with them everything I have. Then I would actually have twelve ministers among the laymen who in turn could take other men and teach them. I know one or two churches that are doing that, and it is revolutionizing the church."

George Martin, in *Today's Parish*, proposes a similar plan to solve the impending priest shortage in the Catholic Church. Martin points to the example of Jesus' training of the twelve and says, "Perhaps pastors should imagine that they are going to have three more years in their parish as pastor—and that there will be no replacement for them when they leave. If they acted as if this were going to happen they would put the highest priority on selecting, motivating and training lay leaders that could carry on as much as possible of the mission of the parish after they left. The results of three sustained years of such an approach would be quite significant. Even revolutionary.''

In recent years many Christians have taken a fresh interest in Jesus' method of training men for ministry, the need to train laymen, the need for Christian leaders who can function as elders in communities—all these factors have been working to turn people's attention to Jesus' relationship with His disciples.

There is a wide variety of interpretations of discipling. Several years ago this subject prompted considerable controversy. Some people have questioned the appropriateness of formation relationships of this sort with anyone besides Jesus Himself. Others have seized upon it as the solution to most of the church's problems.

In this essay I will describe three formation relationships: the rabbi-disciple relationship, the relationship of fathers and sons among the Jews of Jesus' day, and the relationship between leaders of the early church and the men they trained. My goal is to examine a kind of training relationship which is unfamiliar to most of us but which, I believe, has great potential to strengthen the church and Christian family life.

As modern Christians, when we think of disciples, our tendency is to think only of the twelve, Jesus' disciples. But the New Testament also talks about the disciples of the Pharisees and of John the Baptist (Matt. 9:14; 22:15-16; Mark 2:18; Luke 11:1). Among Jews in the time of Jesus, the master-disciple relationship was the ordinary means for preparing men for roles of religious leadership. Though the Greek word for disciple meant simply a student, in the New Testament it always connotes more than this. The disciples referred to in the New Testament were, in their relationship to their teachers, more like apprentices.

Before proceeding further it is worth mentioning that the New Testament also uses the term "disciples" for all who believe in Jesus. So there are two ways in which the word is used: one, for those particular people who follow a master such as Jesus or John the Baptist everywhere, in an explicit apprentice-like formation relationship; and the other for all who accept the gospel and become Christians.

The failure to distinguish these two senses of the word "disciple" has been a source of confusion to many, especially in interpreting Matthew 28: "Go and make disciples of all nations." Some have concluded that every Christian ought to be discipled in the same way the twelve were. Others, seeking to meet the need all new Christians have for formation and instruction, have applied the term "discipleship training" to that basic teaching, to the call to a full commitment or to evangelism training. Consequently they have developed a diluted concept of discipling that bears only a faint resemblance to the relationship of Jesus to His disciples.

Rabbi and Disciples

An excellent source of information on the nature of discipleship at the time of Jesus is a scholarly article entitled "The Relations between Master and Disciple in the Talmudic Age," by Moses Aberbach (see note at end of chapter).

As Aberbach describes it, what is striking about the

rabbi-disciple pattern of education is how learning was so tied to a committed personal relationship between the student and the teacher. Though studying by oneself was not unknown, it was widely looked upon with disapproval, as likely to result in aberrations.

The training that a disciple received from his master included much more than academic study, and went well beyond the classroom. The disciple spent as much time with his teacher as possible, often living with him in the same house. Aberbach says, "Disciples were expected not only to study the law in all its ramifications, but also to acquaint themselves with a specific way of life, which could be done only through constant attendance upon a master....The rabbis taught as much by example as by precept. For this reason the disciple needed to take note of his master's daily conversation and habits, as well as his teaching."

Students related to their masters with deference and respect. To "follow" a teacher meant to accept his teaching, but when accompanying their master, disciples were expected literally to walk behind him, and to one side or the other. Students also served their teacher in many practical ways, ranging from setting up the benches in the room used for instruction to shopping and cooking for him.

Despite the subordination and customs of respect that characterized the master-disciple relationship, it was in no way a distant or merely formal relationship. The teacher attempted to raise his disciples as sons: he cared for them, provided for them (usually this education was at the rabbi's expense), and praised or admonished his disciples as he saw fit. Aberbach describes the relationship as very close and characterized by an intense paternal-filial love. The standard summary of the responsibilities of the disciples was that all the duties normally owed to one's father were owed to one's master.

After completing their term of training, disciples were expected to become teachers themselves and to pass on their master's teaching.

Jesus and the Twelve

When we examine the Gospels in the light of what we know of the rabbi-discipleship relationship, we can recognize much that is familiar. Jesus was concerned that His disciples should learn by being with Him and observing what He did and said. They lived with Him and traveled with Him. It was a relationship of commitment. Jesus' disciples left their families, friends and occupations in order to follow and learn from Him.

It is fairly certain that many of the customs of respect that characterized the relationships of the rabbis and their disciples were true of the relationship of Jesus and the twelve. The Gospels record that Jesus' disciples served Him in a variety of ways: purchasing food, preparing the Passover and paying the temple tax, to name a few instances (John 4:8; Matt. 26:17; Matt. 17:24-27).

We see the same goal in Jesus' relationship with His disciples. He wants them to understand and pass on His teaching, and in a certain sense to take His place. "A disciple...when he is fully taught will be like his teacher" (Luke 6:40). "As the Father has sent me, even so I send you" (John 20:21). "He who hears you hears me, he who rejects you rejects me" (Luke 10:16).

Of course Jesus' relationship with His disciples differed in important ways from other rabbis' relationships with their disciples. He asked more of His followers than any earthly rabbi could have dared to ask. He never intended His disciples to fully take His place: "But you are not to be called rabbi, for you have one teacher, and you are all brethren. And call no man your father on earth, for you have one Father, who is in heaven. Neither be called masters, for you have one master, the Christ" (Matt. 23:8-10). Jesus was instructing His followers to make disciples who would primarily be disciples of Jesus, and only secondarily taught by Peter or Andrew, Apollos or Paul.

To understand Jesus' relationship with the twelve, and formation relationships in general, it is helpful to examine the relationship between fathers and sons among Jews during the biblical period. The father-son relationship provided the model for the rabbi-disciple relationship, and was the formation relationship that shaped Jewish society and gave it continuity and strength.

Among the Jews of the Old Testament, as among the Jews of Jesus' day, the mother cared for, taught and trained both boys and girls during their first few years. But beginning between the ages of five and seven years, the father would take over the primary role in raising the boys.

Boys spent all their time with their fathers. For instance, if a boy's father was a carpenter, the boy would go with his father and help him, doing very simple things when he was young and taking on more and more responsibility as he became older. The son would in that way have the opportunity to observe how the father related to every circumstance in life, as well as to learn his father's trade. The father would teach his son by showing him what he did. Jesus referred to this dimension of the relationship of fathers to their sons when he said,

"The Father loves the Son, and shows him all that he himself is doing" (John 5:20). The father's ideal was to raise up a son who would be like himself.

The Scriptures emphasize the fathers' role in teaching their sons. When God instructs Israel about the Passover, He commands fathers to explain to their sons how the Lord brought them out of Egypt (Ex. 13:14). The father was the primary source of teaching about the family's faith, the history of the people and matters of behavior: "Ask thy father and he will show you" (Deut. 32:7; see also Deut. 6:6-7,20-25; Ex. 13:13-15). The book of Proverbs is full of exhortations to sons to heed their fathers' instruction, and to fathers to teach their sons (Prov. 1:8; 3:1; and elsewhere; Prov. 19:18; 29:17—the word for "discipline" and "correct" here also means to instruct.)

The dialogue between the elder brother and his father at the end of the story of the prodigal son (Luke 15) illustrates the kind of relationship that existed between fathers and sons at the time of Jesus. The elder son objects to the party for his brother and claims that he has been mistreated since "these many years I have served you and obeyed you." These were the obligations a son, even an adult son, owed his father while he was in his house.

The father responds by saying that the circumstances justified the celebration, and that he had not failed in his obligations to his elder son: "Son, you are always with me, and all that is mine is yours." The father had shared his life fully with his son. Already what belonged to the father was virtually his son's possession; and when the father died, the son would succeed fully to his father's position.

"Timothy, My Son"

Whatever insights we have gained into Jesus' relationship with the twelve and the formation fathers gave their sons, a question remains: Is there a place for this intense method of leadership training in the church? Or was Jesus' training of the twelve a unique exercise because the disciples' role in salvation history and in the church was to be unique? Did Jesus' character qualify Him and Him alone to make disciples?

The history of the early church shows that formation relationships like the ones we have been examining were employed by the early Christians. Though the New Testament only once uses the term disciple to describe the relationship of Christians with anyone but Jesus (Acts 9:25), it clearly shows Barnabas training Paul, and Paul training Timothy, Titus and probably others. Of these, Scripture gives us the most information about Paul's relationship with Timothy.

Paul took Timothy from Lystra to travel with him and assist him in his ministry. For a number of years Timothy remained with Paul. During that time Paul sent him on various missions, and finally set him in responsibility over the church at Ephesus. It was to Timothy, the graduate disciple, that Paul addressed the two letters that bear Timothy's name.

Paul regarded Timothy as his son, and Timothy regarded Paul as his father in the Lord (1 Tim. 1:2,18). Paul felt free to issue Timothy commands about governing the church in Ephesus (for example, 1 Tim. 1:3,18; 5:3,9,17). Timothy was under the authority of Paul in his ministry; the church of Ephesus was also under Paul's supervision.

Paul gave Timothy advice about handling various

relations with people, much as a father might counsel his son: "Do not rebuke an older man...treat younger men like brothers, older women like mothers, younger women like sisters, in all purity" (1 Tim. 5:1-2).

Paul gives Timothy personal directions about his health. He doesn't try to persuade Timothy, he simply tells him what to do: "No longer drink only water, but use a little wine for the sake of your stomach and your frequent ailments" (1 Tim. 5:23).

At another point Paul gives a personal exhortation to Timothy about an area of weakness. "Hence I remind you to rekindle the gift of God that is within you through the laying on of my hands; for God did not give us a spirit of timidity but a spirit of power and love and self-control. Do not be ashamed then of testifying to our Lord" (2 Tim. 1:6-8). Timothy, like many of God's servants, had a confidence problem and a tendency not to deal with things in a straightforward manner.

Paul reminds Timothy to continue in the paths that Paul had shown him by his teaching and by his example. "Follow the pattern of the sound words which you have heard from me...guard the truth that has been entrusted to you..." (2 Tim. 1:13,14). "Now you have observed my teaching, my conduct, my aim in life, my faith, my patience, my love, my steadfastness, my persecutions....Continue in what you have learned and have firmly believed, knowing from whom you learn it" (2 Tim. 3:10-14).

Discipleship: The Common Call

At this point it will be helpful to identify the common characteristics of the relationships between rabbis and disciples, fathers and sons, and early church leaders such as Paul and younger pastoral leaders such as

Timothy. This will clarify what I mean by "formation relationship."

First, the purpose of these relationships was to prepare someone for a role similar to that of the person doing the training. Thus sons were prepared for the responsibilities of manhood and fatherhood, and Timothy and the twelve were prepared for roles of Christian leadership.

Second, there was a definite order to the relationships: one person was doing the training. The person being trained served the person who was training him and received personal direction from him. Formation relationships entailed a degree of personal direction beyond normal pastoring.

Third, much of the formation took place through the person doing the training, living and working in the presence of the person being trained. During the time spent together, the person who was giving formation sought to teach by his example, and the person receiving it sought to model himself after his teacher.

Fourth, an important responsibility of the person doing the training is to teach. In all the examples considered in this article, the teaching was about the Scriptures, how to conduct oneself in daily life, and how to do what the trainer did, be it carpentry or pastoring.

Finally, the relationship between the person giving the formation and the person receiving it was deep, close and personal. In these examples, it was analogous to the relationship between a father and a son. Because the purpose of the relationship was formation, the training phase was temporary, though a life-long bond was established, paralleling the relationship of an adult son to his father.

I believe the advantages to formation relationships are obvious. How many sons could benefit from that kind of relationship with their fathers? How many Christian leaders could achieve maturity more quickly and with fewer casualties if this kind of training were practiced? Whatever other arguments could be adduced for their usefulness, the fact that Jesus relied upon formation relationships to train the church's first leaders should motivate us to consider them seriously.

Note: In *Essays Presented to Chief Rabbi Israel Brodie*, Hirsch Jacob Zimmels, J. Rabbinowitz and I. Finestein, editors, Jews' College Publications, New Series No. 3 (London: Soncino Press, 1968).

CHAPTER TEN

One-to-One Pastoral Care: Why and How?

by Bruce Yocum

God has placed men and women in our care with the intention that we should raise them up into His image and likeness. One of the means of doing this is a personal relationship with people to teach and guide them in developing as Christians in every aspect of their lives. Paul defined the goal when he described his ministry to the Colossians as warning and teaching every man "that we may present every man mature in Christ" (1:28).

Not every pastoral relationship involves this kind of care. Often we lead by taking responsibility for activities, by offering teaching and counsel, by setting an example. A one-to-one pastoral relationship in which we have an overall care for someone's personal life is not appropriate in every context. It requires maturity on the part of the pastoral leader, and willing commitment on the part of the person being cared for. We can provide this type of care only to a few people at any one time.

My concern in this essay is not *who* should exercise one-to-one pastoral care, but *how* we should exercise it. To pastoral leaders who have some responsibility for and authority over the personal lives of Christian brothers and sisters (this includes parents caring for their children), I offer some reflections on the elements of one-to-one pastoral care.

Difficult as it often is to bring someone into the Christian life, even more effort is required to help a person grow to be all God wants him or her to be. Farther in Colossians Paul says, "As therefore you received Christ Jesus the Lord, so live in him, rooted and built up in him and established in the faith, just as you were taught, abounding in thanksgiving" (2:6-7). Helping someone who has received the Lord learn to live in Him is a considerable task. Paul says that exercising pastoral care calls for the wisdom and inspiration of God (1:28-29) and involves us in the sufferings of Christ (1:24-25).

It also involves a union of service and authority. Jesus came as One who "emptied himself, taking the form of a servant" (Phil. 2:7), who was "gentle and lowly of heart" (Matt. 11:29), who gave His disciples the example of washing their feet. But Jesus' servanthood did not at all mean that He did not exercise authority. He exercised a great deal of authority; sometimes He even dealt with His disciples severely. Consider the incident in which Peter tried to get Him to change His mind about going to Jerusalem.

While many people today see service and authority as opposites, Jesus combined them. His service to His disciples was to be their Lord, leading them into God's life. His authority over them was always exercised in a way that served them; His pastoral care focused on their needs and their growth in His life. His authority over them was for *their* sake.

On Their Side

An important element of one-to-one pastoral care is to be *for* our brothers and sisters, that is to say, on their side. We ought to have their interests at heart—and be able to express that to them. They need to experience that our desire is for them to become what the Lord wants them to become.

That may seem obvious, but it's not. We can find ourselves, more or less subtly, having almost an adversary relationship with people we care for. We can think and act as if it's "us versus them": Are they going to listen to us or are they not? Are they going to respond to us? Are they going to take our direction? We are on the lookout for rebellion.

Usually that approach comes from our lack of security and our fears about how we are going to be accepted. This can cripple our care for someone. If we are not on the side of the people we are caring for, and if we are communicating that, we will not be in a position to lead them well.

An "us-versus-them" attitude often comes up when someone is having difficulty. But often, when a person is having a hard time responding to pastoral care, it is because of some internal difficulty other than rebelliousness. That is to say, the person has not hardheartedly decided that he is not going to receive advice and counsel, but some kind of fear or confusion or spiritual difficulty is at the root of his problem. If we force things, trying to put down the "rebellion," we may actually stir up rebellion. In fact, the pastoral care relationship may just fade away; before long, we will find ourselves unable to do anything for the person.

Now that is not always the case. Sometimes people actually don't want pastoral authority over their lives, and resist it. When that happens it's sometimes appropriate to deal with their rebelliousness by helping them see that unless they are willing to change their attitude the pastoral leader will not be able to do much for them.

The Power of Affection

We also need to be affectionate with people we're caring for. Expressing affection can make miraculous changes.

Several years ago I had a tough discussion with someone I was responsible for. It was a real head-knocker. We got down to some serious problems that had to get resolved, and the man didn't want to change. In the course of the conversation this man began to get very hostile. I didn't understand. I knew that what I was telling him would make a good change for him if he could just see it. But he couldn't.

All of a sudden a light went on in my mind: "This guy is afraid, that's all. You're working something through with him, and you've brought him to a point where he's facing something inside himself that he's afraid of. He's backing away and getting hostile because of that fear." I felt the Lord saying, "What you should do right now is show him some affection."

Well, this guy was really angry at me. When I began to reach out and put my arm around his shoulder, he grabbed my arm and pushed it away. I tried again. Something began to change. When I put my arm around him, he melted. The hostility disappeared, and he started telling me about what was going on inside him in a very trusting way.

All of our experiences won't be so dramatic, but that was a good illustration of how much difference it can make to express affection. By showing that man some affection I communicated to him, in a way he could understand, that I really cared for him and wanted to help him. He immediately changed and was able to respond to me.

Of course we shouldn't act in an affectionate way toward the people we are responsible for only in a crisis, because if we do, they will not believe or accept it. We need to be consistently affectionate with people.

Correcting, Teaching, Admonition

Another aspect of one-to-one pastoral care is correction. We should not be afraid to correct the people we are responsible for. However, we ought to correct the most important things first, not the things that irritate us most. The reason for this is that when we correct people we teach them our values and priorities.

I can give you an example from my household. It annoys me when people forget to turn off lights. For a long time I tended to correct men in my household for not turning off lights. If they were to have judged by the amount of energy I invested in different forms of correction, they would have had to assume that I believed this was the most important thing that needed to be changed in their lives. I corrected them more quickly when they forgot to turn out lights than when they sinned, because a lot of their sins didn't bother me as much.

Sometimes we don't correct the things most seriously

in need of correction simply because we fail to look beyond the problems we see most easily or which come up the most. We ought to think about the people we are caring for and ask ourselves, "What is out of line here? Where does God want this person to be? What things is he doing that most need to get corrected?" That is where our correction should begin.

Too much correction can be a burden for the people we care for. Perhaps a person has a hundred things in his life that need to change. We shouldn't try to correct everything at once. Better to correct only the things he can actually cope with, and when he changes those, then give him some more.

Correction is closely associated with teaching, which is often neglected. Sometimes the reason people don't respond when we correct them is very simple: they don't know how.

An example of this occurred in my house. I was frustrated about the way chores were getting done. The problem had gone on for a while. I didn't know how to get the men to handle certain things the right way. I would correct them and correct them and correct them.

I was talking to another brother about this, and he said, "Maybe what you need to do is sit down with them and explain how you want them to approach this."

I thought, "Hmm. That's interesting. Maybe that is all I need to do. Maybe I've been getting upset all this time and they simply haven't known what I was really after." Sure enough, that turned out to be the case. All the men needed was a bit of practical instruction, and they were able to respond.

I once read an article about some psychologists who analyzed the way John Wooden coached the basketball team at UCLA. They observed his coaching and classified the various things he said to his players—correcting, instruction, demonstrating, and so on. I was interested to see that he used a variety of kinds of correction.

One was correction with instruction; that is, he would say, "No, don't do it that way; do it this way instead." He wouldn't just say, "Don't do that." He'd also say, "Here's how you're supposed to do it. When they're running this kind of offense, here's where you ought to play."

A slightly different kind of correction he would give was called correction with reinstruction. He would correct the players and teach them again something they already knew. Anyone who has been the parent of a small child will appreciate the value of that. A parent doesn't say to a child, "Here's how you do this," just once. He says to him many times, "Here's how you do this"—and eventually the child learns it.

Adults are the same way. We have to reinstruct them. When we correct people we should keep our eyes open to see when we can give some instruction or reinstruction along with it.

Teaching should not only accompany correction; it should predominate in our exercise of pastoral care.

In some ways, correction is the easiest element of headship. We find it easier to see the things that are wrong and to say, "Stop doing it," than to teach people what it means to be a man or woman of God.

But it's much healthier for a person to be able to say, "What's going on in my life right now is that the Lord is making me this kind of person," than to have to say, "What's going on in my life is that I'm trying to change this, stop that and overcome this other problem." The person's report on what God is doing in his life can make him sound like a patient in a spiritual intensive care unit.

I was working with one man whom I had been correcting for the same fault for about two years—consistently, incessantly. I would say, "You're doing it again. Don't do it." I thought he just had to work on it. I had to keep whacking away at it, until we both, by perseverance and courage, overcame.

Then the Lord intervened. He said to me, "Bruce, do you know what I want to have happen in that brother's life?" I thought about it and I had to say, "I really don't know." I was supposed to be caring for this man's life, helping him get where the Lord wanted him to be, but when the Lord asked me if I knew where He wanted him to be I had to say I didn't. I started asking the Lord where He wanted him to be, and the Lord showed me.

I went to the man and instead of saying, "Stop doing all these things," I said, "This is how you ought to approach things. Live your life this way; handle it this way; do this and do this." It made an amazing difference. A lot of things came into line right away in that brother's life.

One qualification about teaching. A friend of mine expressed it in a proverb he composed at a conference several years ago, where it got a round of applause. He said, "Don't teach what you don't know. Teach only what you know." How often do we try to teach people things we don't really know, or to handle problems that we don't really know how to handle? How much easier to say, "I don't know," and try to find out!

An element of personal pastoral care that is similar to correction is admonition, which means warning.

When you get stopped by a policeman he can either give you a ticket or an admonition. You'd much rather have the admonition.

Admonition usually means warning someone that they are going in the wrong direction and telling them what kind of consequences they can expect. Another aspect of admonition is that we can look at a person's life and see where he might get into difficulty and warn him to be alert to it.

Encouragement

The people in our care also need encouragement. To encourage someone simply means to give them some kind of strength or courage.

Encouragement has to be realistically based. All of us know Christians who are naturally cheerful and go around encouraging everybody about everything. I have noticed that this sometimes does not help much. Here you have this problem to contend with and this person is saying all these cheerful things to you about it. But you know they are not really considering your problem and giving you a solid reason to be encouraged about it. They are just saying what they would say to anybody in that kind of situation.

Some truths are always the case—that God is faithful to us and we can rely on Him. We can encourage people on that basis in any situation. But we should say it in a way that is not glib.

When we encourage people, we should do it in a personal way. It should be something from us to them, not just something we pulled out of our box of scriptural promises that morning. If we tell someone that God is faithful, we should say it in a way that allows him to see that we recommend he rely on God because we know

God is faithful, because we love him and we know that faith will work well for him.

Here is an example of a kind of encouragement we might not ordinarily think of. A man and his son, who had just learned to drive, were driving together, and the son got in an accident. Although nobody was hurt, the car was demolished. It wasn't the son's fault. He might have been able to avoid the accident if he were more skillful, but it wasn't his fault.

They got home, and a little later an errand had to be run. The father got the keys to their second car and gave them to his son and said, "Will you go down to the store and get this thing?"

That made a difference for the young man. He was probably still shaking from the accident. But his father clearly communicated that he trusted him, that he knew the accident hadn't been his fault, and that he ought to go back out and not lose confidence in himself.

He could have spent a lot of time saying, "I want to encourage you. You're a good driver. I know you'll be able to deal with things like this in the future. Don't worry about it." That might not have done nearly as much for the young man as the simple demonstration of trust.

I received what may seem a grim kind of encouragement several years ago. I was tired, worn down by the different things I was doing in the community. I told the man who was caring for me pastorally, "I'm exhausted. It doesn't seem to me I can handle all this." We talked it over.

Now as a matter of fact I couldn't handle it all. And at that time he couldn't take away any of my responsibilities. So what he did was say to me, "Look, I know you can't handle all that. And I can't do anything about it yet. What you need to do is to hang in there, rely on the power of God, and go through it."

That was a big help. I was able to go back saying, "I'm tired, but I know it's okay to be tired. I can't handle all this stuff, but I know it's okay not to be able to handle it all. I know things will be changed as soon as they can be. Meanwhile, I can hang in there and rely on the power of God." My pastoral leader didn't just say to me, "There, there! Things will work out for the good." He was realistic about the situation. But he gave me strength by the way he talked about it.

Practical Help

One-to-one pastoral care often involves some rather unspiritual things.

It can mean helping a person deal with natural life circumstances. If we see someone is in a situation he can't handle, we should help get him out of it. He might not be able to get out of it himself. If we can't change his circumstances, we should do something to support him.

If a man has a job that has him working 14 hours a day, and he can't handle his family and his job, we can try to get him out of the job. If he can't get out of the job, we can provide him some kind of help. Perhaps we can get some brothers and sisters to come over and spend time with his wife and children.

Sometimes we need to give a person material help. We may need to give him money. If we don't have any money to give to him, we should try to find some. Obviously we don't want to give someone money if the reason he does not have it is because he is irresponsible. But many people don't have money simply because they don't have it. They are being as responsible as they can.

We should try to help people's lives to work right. We should find out what needs to get taken care of and help them take care of it.

Sometimes that means spending time with people. Perhaps they need to spend more time with the person who is taking responsibility for their lives, to be in more of a personal relationship with us in order to experience our teaching and encouragement and correction in the right way.

We ought to keep an eye on people's schedules. If they have to do something for the Lord's sake that will hurt them, we can encourage and help them through it. But we shouldn't let people hurt themselves if they don't need to.

It is not at all easy to give one-to-one pastoral care to people. Most of us have not been trained in how to do it. Most of us have not experienced much of it in our lives.

The prospect of having to do something difficult should not discourage us. But it *should* cause us to be patient with ourselves as we grow in our ability to care for people. It takes time to learn how to exercise one-to-one pastoral care. We shouldn't expect to be perfect right away.

We should be humble enough to ask for help when we do not know how to do things. Anyone caring for brothers and sisters should be receiving personal pastoral care himself and should be receiving training in giving pastoral care. If we don't know how to do something, we should not go messing up the person's life; we ought to find out how to do it.

If we stay in touch with those over us about the care we are giving other people, they can take care of us. That will put us in a position to give one-to-one pastoral care in a relaxed, free and confident way.

CHAPTER ELEVEN

Law and Grace

by Stephen B. Clark

Christian leaders who exercise personal pastoral care—such as elders of communities and heads of families—often are not fully effective because they do not adequately understand the practical uses of law and grace. If we are to help the people we are responsible for live the Christian life, we must know how to utilize commands and requirements on the one hand, and encouragement and favor on the other.

Our difficulty with understanding the uses of law is due partly to the influences of our society, which has an ever-decreasing appreciation of authority. Our problem also stems from mistaken notions about Jesus' attitude toward law. Many people cannot see the importance of requiring people to conform to particular standards because they think Jesus rejected law or was very lenient about it. Didn't He purposely break the Sabbath codes, rebuke the people who were well-known for their scrupulous observance of the law, and direct His ministry to those who had fallen short of the law's demands?

Jesus and Law

But the view that Jesus opposed law is a distortion. In the Sermon on the Mount, Jesus says, "Think not that I have come to abolish the law and the prophets; I have come not to abolish them but to fulfill them.... Whoever then relaxes one of the least of these commandments and teaches men so, shall be called least in the kingdom of heaven; but he who does them and teaches them shall be called great in the kingdom of heaven. For I tell you, unless your righteousness exceeds that of the scribes and Pharisees, you will never enter the kingdom of heaven" (Matt. 5:17,19-20).

Clearly, Jesus' attitude toward the law is not negative; Jesus teaches that we must even outdo the scribes and Pharisees, who were noted for their careful observance of the law.

"You have heard that it was said, 'You shall not commit adultery.' But I say to you that everyone who looks at a woman lustfully has already committed adultery with her in his heart" (Matt. 5:27-28).

Jesus is not abolishing the law. He is saying we cannot merely conform ourselves to an external rule, without having an inner intention. We cannot refrain from adulterous behavior while allowing ourselves to desire adultery. Rather, we must have an inner conformance to the external rule.

"Pharisees came up to Him and tested Him by asking, 'Is it lawful to divorce one's wife for any cause?' He answered, 'Have you not read that he who made them male and female shall leave his father and mother and be joined to his wife, and the two shall become one? So they are no longer two but one. What therefore God has joined together, let no man put asunder' " (Matt. 19:3-6).

There were two rabbinical opinions at the time. One was the view of the school of Hillel, which said a man could divorce his wife for virtually any reason. The other was the opinion of the school of Shamia which allowed divorce only for certain strict reasons.

The Pharisees came to Jesus to see where He stood on this issue. Their question can be read in two ways. "Is it lawful to divorce one's wife for merely any reason?" or, "Is there any reason at all for which a man can divorce his wife?"

Jesus shows Himself to be stricter than either school of the Pharisees. But what is crucial is the way in which He is strict. He is not strict in simply demanding external conformance to a rule, but He holds up God's fundamental intentions in this area of human life.

When the Pharisees ask Him about Moses' rule that a man could give his wife a certificate of divorce, Jesus replies that to understand that issue we must grasp God's original intention regarding marriage. Moses' rule was a concession to those who are hard of heart. But if someone wants to handle marriage rightly, he should not claim the law. He should recognize God's purpose: that the two become one.

Uses of Law

A law is a rule for dealing with several situations of the same kind. For example, if a married man is having trouble with his wife, the rule is that he should not divorce her; he should work out the problem in other ways.

Jesus says that rules are good because they express something important about areas of human life. But He teaches that it is not right simply to fulfill the external requirements of the law. We should see what it expresses and set our hearts on that. Our intention should be to fulfill what the law is trying to accomplish.

Jesus directs our attention to the law's fundamental purposes: that we should be like our heavenly Father (see Matt. 5:43-48) and fulfill His plans for creation. These goals are not reducible to a set of laws. Laws can help by excluding some unacceptable behavior, but they are not a complete guide for fulfilling God's purposes.

This positive view of law does not contradict what Paul says. He writes that the law is good, and we cannot disregard it. If we ask, Can we fail to fulfill the commandments? Is it okay to commit adultery now that we're free?, we know Paul's answer: "By no means!" (Rom. 6:1-2).

But he makes a very important point about the law: it is not the means of salvation. In other words, the law is not what brings success to our lives as Christians. It is not the law that gives us relationship with God or that brings us the power to fulfill the standards that God sets for us. These come through the grace of God and faith in Jesus Christ.

Law, then, has a usefulness in pastoral care because it sets minimum standards for behavior and it expresses something of God's intention for our lives. It can do some things to help people live as Christians, but it cannot do everything. Christian pastoral care does not reject rules, commands, discipline and correction. It utilizes them wisely, understanding their uses and limitations.

Practically, there are at least two ways law is helpful. One is that when there is something people have to do, or something they must not do, we should tell them squarely. Making this kind of law clear is an indispensable service. This applies to behavior we know is necessary or unacceptable because God says so, and also to things we decide are necessary or unacceptable in situations we are responsible for.

Another use of law is that sometimes, by making particular behavior a matter of command, we can help people learn to exercise their own will. For example, one of the men under my pastoral care was having trouble controlling his use of time. I taught him and encouraged him about it, but it became clear he needed something more because he continually had to struggle with his will in the area. Finally, we agreed that I would lay down a few things that he would be expected to do. There would be no more discussions, but that these were things he would have to do. At the end of every day he was to tell me if he had done them; if he hadn't he would have to repent for breaking our agreement.

Within two weeks there was a remarkable change. He was able, in effect, to use my willpower to begin to gain control in that part of his life. The time will come when he will no longer need my willpower. The day-and-night difference he experienced illustrates how rules, commands and correction can bring strength into somebody's life from the outside, allowing them to do something they won't do themselves.

Using Law Wisely

When we exercise personal pastoral care, we need to understand not only what it is that law is useful for but also how to use it. Pastoral leaders often face problems regarding firmness, expectations of obedience, strictness and adjustment to a developing headship relationship.

First, let's talk about firmness. Law will not work if we are not firm.

Recently I worked with a man who has several children. The way he related to his children shows what happens when the head is not firm. If he told his young sons he wanted them to stop doing something, they would usually keep doing it. He would ignore them for a while, then he would come back and say again, "I want you to stop doing that." Only after telling them several times would he finally get them to stop.

The boys sensed how far they could get their way. They knew that most of the time they didn't have to listen to their father when he told them what to do, and they didn't want to obey.

The result demonstrates a basic principle about exercising authority. If we are going to give a command or set a rule, we need to be firm about it; otherwise we will lose authority and respect.

We also need to be firm in our promises. The Lord is a perfect example of firmness in all He says, not only in His commands but also in His promises. If He says He is going to give us something, He will give it to us. If we do something wrong, He punishes us if we do it. He instructs us in some qualifications on that, but basically He approaches us with firmness.

We need to distinguish firmness from other qualities it is sometimes confused with. First of all, firmness is not harshness. A person can be both firm and gentle. Firmness is also not the same as anger. We can be firm in a warm, affectionate way. Sometimes anger is appropriate, but we can be firm without it.

It is also important to clarify our expectations regarding obedience. We can approach rules in two ways. One is to require people to obey every rule we lay down. If we do that, we ought not to make a lot of rules. Usually, having many rules either burdens everyone or trains them to disregard our expectations. Normally, we ought to lay down a rule only when we think it is important! And if we expect everyone to obey it, we ought to give time to training people to observe it.

The other approach to rules views them as guidelines or ideals. If we take this approach, we ought to tell people clearly what we are doing. We should let them know which rules they should treat as guidelines and which ones we expect them to obey. Otherwise they will become confused about our directions; it will seem that we are serious about some but not about the others.

A few words are in order about the distinction between firmness and strictness. Firmness means expecting people to obey standards we set. Strictness means setting high or exacting standards.

Our perspective on strictness should be shaped by the example of Jesus who, as I have pointed out, was not lenient. He often required very high standards, which teaches us that holding people to standards can be an important way of loving them. It draws them to be more the people they ought to be. Normally, being easy on people is not the most loving thing, because it means giving up on helping them become the best people they can be.

Of course, *requiring* a lot from people is not the only way of holding them to a high standard. Often we would do better by *encouraging* them to live according to a high standard.

Moreover, we should handle standards of righteousness, orderliness and achievement differently.

The ten commandments are standards of *righteousness*: so is the commandment that we must love one another. Standards of righteousness concern questions such as: How well are we treating our children and our brothers and sisters? Are we being kind to them? Are we serving them?

Standards of *orderliness* involve things such as being on time, keeping things clean, doing our chores.

Standards of *achievement* describe how much we accomplish. How many evangelism contacts do we make? How much do we pray?

There is an important difference, first of all, between standards of righteousness and of orderliness. Usually, standards of orderliness do not concern matters that are intrinsically good or bad.

Suppose, for example, that the head of a household were to post a note on the bulletin board: "Sam is to wash the dishes." If Sam does not wash the dishes, he has not committed a sin. There is no requirement of divine justice that Sam ever has to wash dishes. But it became his responsibility when the head of his household required it of him for the good order of the house.

On the other hand, if Sam murders his brother he has done something intrinsically very wrong. No one had to post a notice saying, "Sam shall not murder his brother." There is something wrong in the very nature of it.

The Lord approaches these two kinds of standards somewhat differently. He holds us to a very high standard of righteousness, but He does not always hold us to a high standard in matters of order. In exercising personal pastoral care it is right for us to be strict regarding righteousness. We are not free to make judgments about how we will approach righteousness. We cannot decide to be strict on murder, but lenient on adultery.

But we don't have to be strict about orderliness. Of course, we want people to be faithful to their responsibilities. But while we might insist that everyone in the house do their chores, we might decide not to insist that everyone be precisely on time for scheduled activities.

As with standards of orderliness, we have options regarding standards of achievement. Holding people to a high standard of achievement can be helpful. But we should ask ourselves what particular people can do, so that the standards we give them call them on rather than discourage them.

Grace

Normally, we think about the grace of God, not about our grace. But the Lord expects us to be gracious, and grace is an important part of our giving personal headship. Basically, grace means favor, particularly when it is not earned and when we are not committed to giving it.

Grace operates in two important ways in respect to law. First, while law is one element of a pastoral relationship, grace should underlie the relationship itself. When we become pastoral heads for people, we ought to give them the relationship freely. They should not have to earn or deserve our care.

It is often said today that Christians should "accept" people. This can mean two very different things. One is that we should not reject people but should love them despite their faults. In that sense, accepting people means to be gracious, to bestow relationships, to offer our love freely, regardless of what the other person is like.

Another interpretation of acceptance is that we should not let the state of a person's life make any difference to us. If someone is leading a thoroughly sinful life and behaving wretchedly toward everyone, we ought still to treat them as though they were living a good life.

This is not what it means to be gracious. The Lord wants us to love people regardless of what they do. But that does not mean that how people live should not make a difference in how we relate to them.

A woman who was having some difficulties with our community once said to me, "The people in the community don't love me. They're always trying to get me to change. They should just accept me the way I am and love me for it." I tried to explain to her that the Lord loved her and was committed to her in her sin. But He did not accept her sin, and He knew it was important for her to change.

Encouragement is the second way grace plays a part in the pastoral relationship. As heads, we should not neglect to present people with the standards they need to live up to; God does point out areas of our lives where we fall short of His standard and there is sin. And we should teach people, telling them what they should do and showing them how to do it. But we also should be an encouragement to those we have responsibility for.

Encouragement comes in various forms. When we live the kind of life that manifests God's own life, others are encouraged to do the same, even without our telling them they ought to. We encourage people to do what is right simply by telling them it is good; we can urge them to it, without making it a matter of command. We can relate what the Lord has done for us, and invite people to read what He did for Christians in the past. We can tell people when they are doing a good job.

There is a correlation between revelation of the law and the gifts of grace. When the Lord gives us the standards for what we are supposed to be, He also gives us the Comforter, the Paraclete, the encourager, the Holy Spirit, who makes it possible for us to do that which He calls us to. The church is built up in His encouragement (Acts 9:31).

The Lord wants us to be paracletes for the people we are responsible for. He wants us to stand by them. He wants them to experience us as a source of strength, help and encouragement in living their lives as Christians.

Part IV

WHEREVER EIGHT OR TEN ARE GATHERED...

Small groups have come to play an increasingly important role in the life of many churches and communities. Their versatility makes them useful for everything from evangelism to leadership training, and their informality makes them a helpful bridge between the individual and the larger body.

This section discusses small groups primarily as a tool for pastoral care, a way to help Christians lead each other to maturity.

CHAPTER TWELVE

The Theory and Practice of Small Groups

by Kevin Springer

Many church communities have small groups—cell groups, growth groups, home groups, sharing groups, call them what you will. A lot of churches find them helpful for giving everyone a place to belong in church life, for evangelism, for mutual support. But some churches run into difficulties with small groups.

Why? What makes the difference? Is there a formula for success?

No, there are no formulas. Why? Because there is not just one kind of small group.

If there is one common problem in getting small groups to work right in congregations and communities, it is the failure to recognize this diversity. If we are going to have small groups that make a contribution to the life of the church community, we must think carefully about the particular purposes of the groups that we are setting up, and what investment will be necessary for them to succeed.

A useful pastoral exercise is to consider the very range of small-group options that are available, their respective strengths and weaknesses, and what it takes to accomplish their objectives. The way we put them together depends on what we are trying to do. An approach that works well for one purpose may not work well—or may even be counterproductive—for another.

The accompanying chart offers a helpful way to think about small groups. Across the top it lists some of the more common types of small groups. Along the left side it identifies some of the factors to be considered in putting together any small group.

Please note that this is in no way intended to be an exhaustive or comprehensive list. The chart simply tries to present a number of small-group models to illustrate the range of options that are available and the kinds of factors we need to consider. It is not so much intended to answer questions as to stimulate fruitful thinking.

Let's see how the chart works as a tool for thinking about small groups. First, let's look at the different purposes of small groups.

What Sort of Group?

While the New Testament does not offer a treatise on small groups, its descriptions of the early church and its teaching about Christian living give us some insight into the reasons for having small groups. We see the church meeting in small groups in the homes of Priscilla and Aquila, Nympha, and John Mark's mother (Rom. 16:5; Col. 4:15; Acts 12:12). This pattern would have been natural in light of the early Christians' understanding of Christian living. How could they carry each other's burdens (Gal. 6:2) if they were not familiar enough with each other to know what difficulties each person was dealing with? How could they spur one another to love and good works (Heb. 10:24) or look out not only for their own interests but for each other's (Phil. 2:4) if they did not regularly see each other and talk about their lives with each other? How else could they warn the idle, encourage the timid and help the weak (1 Thess. 5:14)? Gatherings in small groups helped serve this purpose in the early church and can do so today.

From the New Testament, then, we might say that the general purpose of small groups is to enable us to live the Christian life together. But in order to set up any particular small groups, we need to be more specific. What aspects of Christian life together are we especially trying to foster? This is where the top row of the chart comes in.

Task-Oriented Groups. These groups come together to perform specific tasks: to provide music at worship services, for example, or to plan monthly social events, or pray with people in the church who are sick. We may not think of these teams or committees as small groups, but in reality that is what they are. The members can have a considerable impact on each other as they work together. I know one man who joined the team providing music for worship on Sunday morning and experienced a significant boost in his self-esteem through the healthy relationships he developed with the other members of the group.

Neighborhood Evangelism Groups. Many of us have had experience with this kind of small group. Often utilizing a simple Bible-study format, they can be a very effective way to reach out to new people.

The church I helped pastor in Port Huron, Michigan, set up evangelistic small groups last year. Looking back, it seems as though for once our spiritual timing was perfect. At the first meeting of the evangelistic home group I led, I asked everyone to share what they were expecting from the meetings. One woman said she had always wanted to have a personal relationship with Jesus Christ and was hoping that someone could tell her how! A couple said they had been looking for a long time for people who could help them understand what the Bible is all about. Needless to say, the series of meetings were a great success.

Fellowship Groups. This is what comes to mind for most of us when we hear the words "small groups." Their goal is simply to bring people together in a regular way to strengthen relationships and foster brotherly and sisterly support. They are often used to help personalize a large church and to help new people feel more at home in a rapidly growing church.

Pastoral Care Groups. Small groups can be an excellent vehicle for providing personal pastoral care for individuals. For example, we can put together a group of men who are being cared for by a particular pastoral leader. The group meets regularly under that pastoral leader's guidance for teaching and personal sharing. Such an approach helps the pastoral leader stay in touch with those under his care and also fosters mutual care and support among the group members themselves.

By creating a network of pastoral care groups in the church, we can structure a way to provide care for all or many of the members of the church. Establishing such groups opens opportunities for middle-level pastoral leadership and creates an excellent training ground for leader development.

Leadership Training Groups. Small groups can be a very effective way to impart teaching and give hands-on guidance to those being prepared for leadership. The greatest example of such a group, of course, was Jesus' training of the twelve!

Key Characteristics

What characteristics do we need to take into account as we think about forming small groups for any of these purposes? Let's consider how the key characteristics vary according to the purpose of the small group. Just as temperature, precipitation and wind direction are parameters of the weather, these are parameters of small groups in the church.

Leader's Gifting and Maturity. The question here is, What level of personal maturity and range of gifts are required to lead this group? Most kinds of small groups do not need a superstar leader. They can be effectively led by the average church member. However, pastoral care groups and leadership training groups must be led by persons with more developed gifts, persons of maturity and solid character.

While the requirements vary according to the type of group, in general a small group leader should evidence the qualities prescribed for all Christian leaders in such passages as 1 Timothy 3:1-7 and Titus 1:5-11. Remember, of course, that we are not looking for perfection! But basic soundness of character is important.

A small group leader should be adept at interpersonal relationships: able to call a group together and keep a discussion on track, able to relate to different kinds of people, able to deal with the kinds of minor personality clashes that sometimes crop up. Of course, the abilities needed along this line vary according to the type of group—less for a task-oriented group, more for a pastorally oriented one.

Every small group leader, of whatever type of group, must be able to be subordinate to the overall church leadership in his service. A small group is meant to be a cell in the larger organism of the church or community, not a separate organism with a life of its own. The fidelity of the leader is the best insurance against the small group becoming distanced from the larger body.

A final, somewhat different, question to ask as we consider the kind of leadership that is required for various types of small groups is, How much time does it take? The small group leader must have adequate time to invest in his service. We often make the mistake of saying, "Just have Joe be the leader. He's a member of the group, so he's going to be there anyway...." For some kinds of groups—fellowship groups, say—that might work. But to the extent that the leader will have to oversee practical arrangements, attend training sessions, and so on, he or she will need to make a larger time investment than the other members of the group.

Training Needed by Leader. How much special instruction and oversight must be given to a person before he can lead the group? Someone leading a task-oriented group needs skills in the area of service—which might be considerable or slight, depending on how technical the area is. The person leading a fellowship group needs only some basic guidance; the one heading a leadership training group may, depending on the situation, require formal education.

Quality of Relationships Among Members. What level of personal affinity and commitment is required for the group to serve its purpose? In a task-oriented group, relationships are largely functional: people only need to relate to each other well enough to get the job done smoothly. In evangelistic and fellowship groups, we are looking for a somewhat deeper quality of relationship: we want the people to get to know each other, to take an interest in each other's needs and problems, to enhance each other's strengths.

For a pastoral care group to serve its purpose, the members must be committed to maintaining strong personal relationships. We cannot expect people to bring serious areas of their lives into the light, and to seek pastoral advice and direction, without some confidence that the others in the group are committed to them. This is even more the case in a leadership training group, where the bond of trust and loyalty with the group leader is especially important.

Schedule Priority. Just how important is it that people attend the meetings regularly? For some small groups, it is not a big problem if people miss occasionally. But other kinds of groups cannot function well unless almost everyone is there almost all the time. Members of these groups need to accept that the small group takes precedence over all but the most pressing outside demands.

Frequency. How often should the group meet? Almost all small groups need to meet *regularly*, but the frequency can vary: weekly, biweekly, monthly. The main variable here is how much you want the group to accomplish, and how quickly.

Longevity. Over what period of time is this group expected to meet? Some need to stay in operation only for a specific period of time. Others require a more open-ended commission if the right kinds of relationships are going to develop.

Some evangelistic small groups, for instance, do best when they are planned to last only a certain length of time. If people know something will run only for four or six or eight weeks, they are more inclined to join in.

Composition. There are two separate considerations here.

The first is, Does the group need to be homogeneous as to sex, age, state in life or other factors? Or will it benefit from mixing some of these elements?

The second is, How long should any particular grouping of individuals expect to stay together?

On both counts, there seems to be more flexibility with task, evangelism and fellowship groups. Pastoral care and leadership training groups need a higher degree of homogeneity and stability to function effectively.

Getting Started

Here are some steps that can be followed in successfully launching small groups.

We should start by *deciding what kind of small groups we want*, taking into consideration such things as God's call to us as a church or community, the present needs of our members, and so on. (Incidentally, there is nothing that says we have to settle on one and only one model. Most churches and communities can benefit from having several different kinds of small groups available.)

The next step is to *assess our resources realistically*.

First, do we now have, or can we raise up, adequate leadership for the groups? A very common mistake is to launch small groups without making adequate provision for their leadership. Asking for volunteers usually is not enough. We need to exercise pastoral judgment in selecting appropriate people.

Second, can our people sustain the additional time and energy demands of small group involvement? Most churches find they cannot simply add small group participation to members' already busy lives, but need to eliminate or de-emphasize other elements of church life to make room for small groups.

There is, of course, an interplay between our needs and our resources. Most of the time we will find ourselves coming at the question from both directions at once, simultaneously balancing what we would like to do against what we seem to be able to do. Flexibility is crucial.

It is important to remember, as we go about developing small groups, that *leaders must be members, too.* It is unwise, and maybe even unfair, for pastoral leaders to try to get their people to do something successfully until they themselves have had some first-hand experience with it and have developed a workable model.

Once we are clear on what to do and how we plan to go about it, we need to *teach the whole congregation about the theory and practice of small groups*. We need to establish the scriptural rationale for small groups and impart a vision of what they can accomplish. People need to understand the particular approach we are adopting and how it will impact their lives: What options are available? What commitments will be expected? We should allow time to resolve questions that arise and to factor into our planning comments and suggestions that are offered.

Finally, we should *start smart*. This means, first of all, starting small. It is wiser to set a modest initial goal and reach it than to frustrate ourselves and our people by setting an unrealistically grandiose goal and falling short.

"Starting smart" also means starting with those who show the greatest desire for the new idea and who, in our pastoral judgment, have the strongest likelihood of making it work. Once we have developed a working model with a good track record, it will be easier to expand the program and bring others into it.

If we begin with a clear idea of the purposes of the groups we are setting up, make sure we are willing and able to pay what they cost, and approach the endeavor with the wisdom born of experience, we will find that small groups can greatly strengthen the life and mission of our church or fellowship.

CHAPTER THIRTEEN

Focus for Small-Group Discussion

by Mike Guenther

Needed: A way to help people who have experienced renewal stay renewed.

Criteria: A method that gets at the basics—fostering personal commitment to Christ and obedience to Him. A method that is widely accessible—workable for people with different backgrounds, education, occupations and responsibilities.

I suspect all of us who have been involved in evangelism and spiritual renewal programs have seen this need and would agree on the criteria. Actually, there is no one solution. But I have found a particular tool that helps meet the need and fits the qualifications. The tool is a format for discussion in small groups.

The groups are set up by a pastoral leader and usually consist of four to six people. The members commit themselves to meet regularly as a group—at least every other week—in order to encourage one another in their lives as Christians. They promise to relate to one another in trust, and to treat what they talk about in confidence. My experience has been that it is more fruitful for men and women to meet in separate groups.

Now, at least to my observation, it is not enough for a group of people to commit themselves to simply talking over their Christian lives and meeting frequently. It is also important to establish in advance what areas of their lives are to be discussed and then to see that this happens.

My goal has been to make sure that the conversation is centered on each person's relationship with the Lord. The group's time together can too easily become confined to discussing jobs, children's problems, current events and the like. I have also been concerned that the discussion be personal, that is, about each person's own life, and not just a theoretical discussion of religious matters. At the same time, it is undesirable for the sessions to become dumping grounds for personal problems.

With these considerations in mind, I have found it effective to orient the conversation around a set of prescribed questions.The particular questions enable each member of the group to share how he is handling certain fundamental commitments as a Christian. Whenever the group meets, each person goes through the list of questions. He or she answers each of them candidly and forthrightly. Of course, this does not prevent the group from taking time together either before or afterwards to talk about other things, such as jobs and children.

Here are the particular questions with a brief explanation and some comments:

1. Have I come before the Lord faithfully in personal prayer and Scripture study?

A fundamental element of the Christian life is the commitment to spend time with the Lord regularly. This commitment can be difficult for someone who has no previous experience with regular, individual prayer and Scripture study. It can also be a challenging commitment for the mature Christian to maintain.

The question is not concerned with whether prayer has been "successful." Instead, it asks simply about faithfulness—whether the person is fulfilling this basic commitment. Also, the question is stated in terms of "coming before the Lord." This emphasizes a basic attitude of acknowledging who God is and who we are before Him. Finally, the question emphasizes the "personal" element. The intent here is to stress the importance of being alone with the Lord.

This question helps people maintain the right kind of relationship with the Lord. It helps people realize that their commitment to pray and read the Bible cannot be satisfied by something else, like good intentions or even "holy activities." The question is also valuable in clarifying priorities. And it is useful in helping people overcome practical difficulties, such as finding the right time or place to practice devotions.

2. Have I fulfilled my responsibilities to the Lord without complaining?

This question helps us look at how we are handling the things the Lord has given us to do. The focus is not on our own needs or desires but rather on responding in the right way to the Lord's action in our lives. In short, we try to see our various responsibilities—such as our jobs or raising our children or serving in some capacity in the church—as work entrusted to us by the Lord.

The question asks if we have done these things without complaining. Here again the emphasis is not on achievement but on approach—on having the heart of a servant, on doing what the master asks without complaint or question.

I have found that this admonition about complaining has helped many people handle their responsibilities with a much different attitude. The question helps us to see more clearly that the Lord has given us an opportunity to serve Him in His work. This is really a cause for thanksgiving. This perspective often enables people to get free from problems like self-pity and, in fact, to become more effective in what they do.

3. Have I conducted myself righteously in thought, word and action?

The purpose of this question is to help us to live our lives "in the light," having an appropriate openness and accountability to our brothers and sisters. It is important that we put into practice the commitments we have made, that is, that we do the right things. It is also obvious that we need to stop any wrongdoing. The discussion of whether we are living righteously helps us to be honest about our lives and to face up to any areas where changes or repentance need to occur.

The question should not be seen as a substitute for other forms of repentance, seeking the Lord's forgiveness, and being reconciled to those we have wronged. Rather, it is intended to help us confront the facts when repentance or change is necessary.

Many people need the support of a few trusted friends in order to break out of bad habits or wrong patterns of conduct. Sometimes they also need help in recognizing that they even have such problems. Wrong ways of speaking about other people, resentments, substance abuse (especially of alcohol) and sexual immorality are examples of problems that people often need to face and deal with.

I have also noticed that this question can benefit people who are hounded by scrupulosity. This is especially true in the area of dealing with unsolicited temptation. They are often helped appreciably by having the perspective and encouragement of others in distinguishing between temptation and actual wrongdoing.

4. Have I responded to God's Word in Scripture and to the leading of the Spirit?

The purpose of this question is to train us to watch for the guidance of the Lord. We want to be receptive to what the Lord may be telling us, both in Scripture and in the events of our daily lives. This question helps us be more attentive to what the Lord may be saying to us. It also requires us to consider whether we are responding.

The question helps all of us to be more conscious of God's action in our own lives. This is essential if we are ever to embrace all that He has for us. Also, by hearing how the Lord is leading others, we can become more conscious of what He is doing with us. Finally, the discussion of this question with the group protects a person from mistaking other things for the leading of the Lord.

Putting the questions on a card that fits in a wallet or purse can be helpful. A person can then look at them during the week and think about answering them at the next meeting.

5. Do you brothers or sisters have any advice for me?

The purpose of this question is to enlist the support and assistance of the other members of the group. The terms "brother" or "sister" are intentional; they emphasize our shared life in Christ.

The objective is not to replace more traditional forms of spiritual direction or to invite in-depth counseling. The question simply provides a practical vehicle for members of the group to support one another. It also provides a means for helping an individual member deal with practical problems.

For example, one man acknowledged that he was not being faithful to his personal prayer. The input of the other members of the group helped him to see that the problem was caused by his trying to pray "on the run." He was encouraged to reorder his priorities and set aside a specific time so that he could be more faithful to his commitment.

In another case, a man expressed his concern over the fact that he consistently experienced sexual temptations whenever he stayed at a particular hotel on business trips. One of the men in the group suggested he consider staying at a different hotel whenever he was visiting that city. It turned out that this suggestion took care of the problem.

In summary, the use of these questions makes the group's interaction more effective. The individuals concentrate on those particular subjects that are essential to being Christian. They are not diverted or distracted by other things they may have in common. The questions also encourage each of the members to live their lives "in the light." In addition, the process of answering these questions together actually provides an experience of sharing in one another's Christian commitment.

Finally, this kind of format can accommodate a diverse group of people. Because it does not draw on common business, social or educational backgrounds, it can be used by everyone.

Usually the results of using this kind of structured discussion are not apparent for several months. Typically what happens is that members of the group realize gradually that they have given substance to their commitment to one another. They have in fact begun to share their lives in Christ. The consequence commonly is to strengthen them in their own relationship to the Lord and in their willingness to lay down their lives for others.

CHAPTER FOURTEEN

What Do Small-Group Leaders Look Like?

by Suzanne Springer

Editor's note: Although this essay discusses small-group leadership in terms of women's small groups, the principles it sets forth are applicable to small groups of all kinds.

Andrea has been leading a women's small group in her church for three years. She does not feel that she can continue much longer, because every time there is a conflict between her and another woman in the group, Andrea goes into depression.

Sally, on the other hand, is very happy as the leader of a small group of women in her community. Although leading the group adds to her busy life, she handles her responsibilities well, and the women find the group a source of strength.

Sally is succeeding where Andrea is having difficulty. Why? What are the qualities and skills that go into being an effective leader of a women's small group?

Pastoral leaders who are setting up women's small groups in the church or fellowship need to consider carefully which women they are placing over the groups. A failure to do this, resulting in ill-suited leaders, can create disasters in women's small groups.

I have found that the following attitudes and marks of character should be present in the life of a woman if she is going to lead others.

1. *A leader needs spiritual and emotional maturity.* She needs to be an example to other women. She need not be perfect, but her spiritual life should be something other women can aspire to. She should have an alive relationship with the Lord, and not be afraid to lead out in prayer, Scripture reading and sharing in group situations. Her speech should encourage others.

When encountering personal difficulties or problems in relationships, she trusts God and communicates a faith in Him to others. For example, one leader I know was going through a miscarriage that lasted weeks. From day to day and week to week she drew on the strength of the Lord, seeing Him as faithful to her and in control of the situation. In difficulty she grew in strength and was an inspiration for others to look to God for help and comfort.

Related to spiritual strength is emotional strength. Andrea did not possess the emotional strength to handle the pressures of leadership. She brooded over and rehashed every conflict in her mind until she became depressed. When wronged by other women she was not able to work it through and let go.

2. *An effective leader's life is in good order.* For a married woman this starts with proper respect and honor

for her husband and pastoral leader. If she has children, they should be under control, not wild banshees. If a woman is failing in these crucial areas, she forfeits any chance for recognition as a leader by other women. Respect for husband and control over children are especially important if a woman leads married women. Also, if a married woman's husband does not support her in a leadership role, she will not be able to win the confidence of women in her group.

Part of having her life in good order is being in good physical condition in areas that she can control, such as weight and exercise. This is not to conform to Madison Avenue's ideal of a beautiful woman, but simply to reflect a personal discipline that is honoring to the Lord.

A leader's personal manner—how she carries herself in social situations—should also be one of dignity and humility. This is especially true of her speech: off-color humor, teasing or a chiding tone are out of place. Her speech patterns will be picked up by those whom she leads—for better or worse.

The way a woman dresses communicates something about her. Dressing with a degree of taste indicates a woman's sense of self-respect also. Does the woman wear appropriate clothing for different situations? Casual clothes worn at a formal church wedding do not show respect for the dignity of either the wedding couple or the wearer.

Adequate neatness and cleanliness of the woman's house are another aspect of order in her life. It is certainly not the case that a woman must be a domestic expert and keep an immaculate home. But other women will find it hard to follow the lead of a woman who does not do a decent job caring for her home. (There is also a valuable modeling factor here.)

When these sorts of things are in order, a woman grows in self-confidence. If the leader does not have self-confidence, it is difficult for others to have confidence in her and it is hard to build others' confidence in themselves. If a woman's life is in order, other women find it easier to trust what she says.

3. *A leader should be honest about herself.* Women need to see into their leader's heart and find an openness to share her life and time with others. Christine, a leader I know, is a beautiful example of this openness. Christine had gained too much weight during her pregnancy, so she joined a weight management group. She lost and kept off the undesired pounds, and her example of acknowledging her problem and seeking help has encouraged other women in her community to seek help unashamedly in this area also.

Sally, the leader mentioned at the beginning, is able to talk with her sisters about her struggles in an appropriate way and ask for prayer, and the other women in turn open their difficulties to her. Together they often discover God's answers to their questions. Often it is Sally's experience as an older sister that leads the way to solutions.

Being honest and transparent means being a good listener. Leaders are not required to have all the answers, but by listening they lend support and often can point others to the place to receive the right answers. Listening is especially important in leading women.

By her open manner, a leader creates an atmosphere where competition and cattiness give way to comradeship. A leader desires to see the success of others.

True sisterhood of caring and supporting one another flourishes under this kind of leadership.

4. *A leader is a bridge builder.* A women's leader is able to help relationships flourish not only between herself and others but among the women in her group. She also needs to be able to deal with conflict. Sometimes dealing with conflict is as routine as coordinating everyone's schedules; sometimes it is more serious and complex. The leader of women neither creates nor avoids conflict but simply deals with it when it arises.

Spiritual and emotional maturity, an openness and honesty of heart, a life in good order, an attitude of respect, humility and dignity, an ability to foster friendships and most importantly a love for the Lord—all these are marks that a potential leader of a small group of women should have. With these traits she can lead others in growing in godly sisterhood.

Part V

CHRISTIAN COMMUNITY

If Christians are to grow to maturity and have a lasting impact on the society around them, the church must be more than a religious organization. It must become a total environment, in which committed personal relationships of love and trust undergird a thoroughly Christianized way of life.

The essays in this section analyze the breakdown of community in secular society, and discuss ways in which pastoral leaders can restore its key elements among their people.

CHAPTER FIFTEEN

The Quiet Passing of Natural Community

by Peter S. Williamson

The way most people live has changed more since the American Revolution than it did in the previous 1700 years or 3700 years. This process of change, if uninterrupted, is likely to produce even greater changes in the next fifty years. I am not referring to the astounding advance in technology, though that is certainly important. Instead, I am referring to radical social change, the transition from a traditional and communal society to a technological society that approaches personal relationships differently from the way they were approached through all of human history. It is immensely important that pastoral leaders understand the changes that are taking place, for they have significant implications for the life of the church.

The Way We Were

By "traditional society" I mean the social patterns and way of life that prevailed everywhere from the beginning of civilization until the last two or three centuries, and that remain in some places even today. Vast differences exist among traditional societies; one has only to think of the broad differences between Chinese, Islamic and medieval Christian societies. However, these and most traditional cultures still held a number of characteristics in common.

Most cultures before our technological age could be called relationship-centered cultures because of the priority personal relationships had in people's lives and in the structures of society. Family life, for instance, was much stronger and more extensive. The family included not only a husband, wife and their offspring, but often an extended household including more than two generations, and sometimes people who were not physically related at all.

Also, kinship relationships were very important. In most cultures, kinship loyalty was strong. The responsibility family members had for even distantly related kinsmen is startling compared to the way those relationships work in the modern world.

Life in pretechnological societies was more communal than it is today. Rural villages and city neighborhoods were characterized by a sense of common identity and by frequent interaction among people. Often work was organized in a communal way, with sowing, harvesting or shepherding being carried out together by a number of families.

Communal festivals, secular and religious, were normal elements in people's lives. These celebrations expressed and reinforced relationships outside the immediate family.

Pretechnological cultures assigned roles to subgroups

within society. For instance, there were clear differences between the responsibilities of young and old and of men and women. These distinctions provided a necessary division of labor to meet the demands of everyday life and provided a sense of identity, security and respect for each person.

For instance, the aged had an important role in passing on the wisdom and tradition of the preceding generations. They taught the younger members of the family and imparted confidence and security. The older men governed the community, and within the family the father normally exercised considerable authority over the activities and lives of its members.

People conceived of themselves as part of their family, village, guild or neighborhood, rather than individualistic terms. It went without question that decisions made by the group formed their life. Thus, Paul could confidently address the Philippian jailer, "Believe in the Lord Jesus, and you will be saved, you *and your household*" (Acts 16:31).

Society consisted of an amalgamation of cohesive groups with their own social structures, whether the groupings were those of kinship, village or neighborhood. The basic units of society were communal groups, rather than individuals.

Within these groups strong human relationships provided a stability that reinforced the stability of society. There was greater predictability than today; fewer changes, fewer options and less mobility—socially, economically, occupationally, geographically.

To be sure, there were exceptions, periods of displacement due to war or natural disasters. There were hardships that many people in the modern world don't experience—the absence of scientific medical care, for instance. We should not romanticize the past. An ultimate evaluation of traditional society as compared with our own would be very difficult to make, and would depend on the values underlying the analysis. Nevertheless, what I have said describes fairly accurately some of the sociological aspects of most traditional cultures.

Technological society is strikingly different from the traditional cultures of the past. The meaning of the word "family" has narrowed to mean the nuclear family, a man and woman and their offspring. Kinship relations quickly lose their importance as people move from place to place to pursue educational or job opportunities. With few exceptions, towns and neighborhoods cease to be characterized by any significant degree of personal relationship among their members.

Technological society is advancing rapidly and touches virtually every country of the world. Though some places have not yet experienced the social changes I am describing, nowhere is change proceeding in the opposite direction.

Technological Man

French lawyer and theologian Jacques Ellul has offered an interpretation of the essential difference between traditional and technological societies. He finds the root difference in technological society's reorientation of human life around technique and results.

A technique is an activity carried out in accordance with a particular method to achieve a particular goal. Sawing wood could be considered a technique since it is an operation that has been developed to accomplish the goal of putting wood into a more useful form. In a different realm, an elementary school is an example of a more complex technical activity. It is a means that relies on a combination of technical activities to educate a large number of children.

Technical action is a way of getting things done. As techniques multiply and are improved, there are more and more results, and more and more is produced or accomplished.

Technical activity has existed for all of history. Anthropologists sometimes speak of three forces that shape culture: social structure, ideology (the beliefs and values of a particular people) and technology. Ellul points out that technology has achieved a dominance in shaping society that it never had before.

Consequently, human life is gradually being functionalized, that is, restructured to maximize effectiveness at accomplishing tasks. Some important dimensions in people's relationships with one another are getting lost in the process.

A comparison illustrates the functionalization of human relationships. The assembly line at an automobile plant is an extreme instance of human activity and relationships being systematically fitted to maximize effectiveness at a particular task. The men who work on assembly lines may have friendships with one another, but the primary reason they are together is to assemble automobiles. Their relationships are completely subordinate to the task at hand. Auto production will continue, while the individual men come and go; the men are interchangeable.

Compare this with what is almost the only remaining communal grouping in technological society, the family. Within the family, goals are accomplished and services exchanged, but anyone who would analyze the family in those terms alone does not understand what family life is all about. The husband is present in that situation simply because it is his family—his wife and his children. The members are there simply because they have a particular relationship with one another. One family member could not be exchanged for another human being of the same sex and same age, in the same way someone on an assembly line could be replaced.

This comparison illustrates the difference between groupings based on function and those based on relationship. In society at large, with the advance of technology, more and more of human life is organized to accomplish things, and personal relationships are increasingly subordinated to functional considerations, as on the assembly line.

The Cost of Effectiveness

It's easy to see ways in which the desires for, and opportunities for, greater effectiveness in achieving results have produced situations that have changed how people relate to one another.

Hospitals can be more effective than the home in taking care of the sick and dying, so that's where they are cared for. Children used to receive their primary training and preparation for adult life from their parents and other family members. Now public schools have gobbled up the lion's share of the job. In traditional society financial support for older members of the family often came from the labor of their children and other relatives. Now that support comes primarily from social welfare programs and pensions from former employers.

Take another example—shopping. In the past, buying food and other items was done at markets or shops or at the homes of the people who produced the goods being purchased. People knew the people they did business with; there was some personal relationship between buyer and seller. In technological society people do much of their shopping in supermarkets or large department stores. Our modern approach is more effective: larger stores provide greater variety and better prices. But in the process, another aspect of human life is functionalized and, in this case, depersonalized.

Today people rarely make their living in their homes. The places where people live have been separated from the places where they work. We may not realize how radical a shift this is; but until the last few hundred years most people's businesses operated out of their homes. Work was not so separated from personal relationships in one's life.

The way that our economy works makes it very valuable for people to be mobile, able to move to wherever they will fit most effectively into the corporate and economic system. People have always moved to different places for economic reasons, but never have people changed where they live on the scale made possible by modern technology. The average American family is reported to change residence once every four years.

This has profound effects on the way people experience human relationships. It weakens all ties outside the nuclear family, since personal relationships depend heavily on geographical proximity. The lack of continuity and stability in personal relationships conditions people to approach relationships with more limited commitments and expectations.

Let me make it clear that I do not advocate a return to the "good old way" of doing things in all these areas. I am simply trying to illustrate how much of human life has been functionalized—organized to maximize effectiveness—and how much natural community is thereby undermined. But there's more.

Another result of functionalizing human relationships is that competence at performing tasks becomes one of the highest values. In technological society, people come to be viewed primarily as bearers of particular skills or abilities. Age and position due to birth or family role are increasingly devalued. So, for example, old age is comparatively little valued because old people are past the peak of their achieving years.

Social control does not disappear from technological society. Instead of an individual exercising personal authority over an extended family household or clan, social pressure and the media now exercise control. When individuals cease to belong to a community, they lose the social context for their values and become vulnerable to pressures and influences, particularly when belief and value changes are gradually introduced through the means of media.

The ultimate outcome of a functionalized approach to human relationships is the atomization of society. Society becomes an aggregate of individuals rather than a network of groups. Even the nuclear family, the last outpost of communal life in technological society, is under pressure to release its individual members: the children to school and community activities and peer groups, the parents to careers and outside interests.

Erosion of Christian Life

The erosion of natural community and strong bonds among groups of people in technological society has taken its toll on church life. The geographical parish, characteristic of the Roman Catholic Church and some

Protestant churches, depends for its community life upon strong bonds among the members of the parish because they live in the same town or section of the city or because they form a distinct cultural group in the larger metropolis. As natural bonds of community are broken down, cohesiveness, mutual care and responsibility, and sharing of life drop away from parish life.

The more common Protestant model of church life, the congregation, might have stood a better chance of fostering strong relationships among its members because it is smaller and because people choose to be a part of a particular church. However, except in the case of tightly knit churches such as some Bible and Pentecostal churches, Protestant churches usually fail to provide community relationships for their members.

The main reason for this is that technological society trains its members to make limited commitments—commitments to attend certain activities and perform certain tasks. Modern Christians attend church with a sense of responsibility and with the hope of receiving certain benefits. They rarely regard the people in the church as people with whom they share their lives. Their friendships, their personal lives, their interests, may coincide with some of the people and activities at church, but they also may not. In this sense Christians approach their commitment to their churches as they would approach commitment to their jobs.

The limited commitment modern Christians make to their churches stands in contrast to the full personal commitment they make to their families and to the full commitment the Christians of the early church made to one another.

The Christian church grew up in the midst of a

traditional society. The society was characterized by a communal, rather than a functional approach to human relationships.

When a person joined the early church, the kind of relationship he had with the other members of the church was not totally new for him. If he was a Jew he was familiar with the commitment and responsibility the Jews viewed themselves as having toward one another. If he was a Greek, he was accustomed to committed relationships with the members of his extended household or his neighbors. Becoming a Christian raised the standard of how he should relate to the people he was committed to; it also changed who it was he was committed to, extending his commitment and responsibility to all who were members of the church.

We know from the New Testament that the early Christians clearly saw themselves as a people: a distinct social unit, brothers and sisters, fellow members of the "body of Christ"—a term which aptly expresses their interrelatedness. They used the word *koinonia* to describe the shared life they had with one another; they were responsible for one another's needs.

Restoring Community

Though technological society presents the church with many new challenges, there is none as important or as difficult as establishing a community relationship among contemporary Christians.

In past ages people's lives were shared with and committed to their kinsmen or neighbors, and they hardly thought about it. It was a fact of life, a given. Today Christians must break with the predominant cultural pattern of making only partial commitments and choose to make full commitments of their lives to one another.

This kind of committed relationship among Christians not only runs contrary to the structure of modern society and the pattern of personal relationships it produces, but it also contradicts ideals of individualism and independence so prevalent in our society. Christians need to set aside these values of the world and take on instead the biblical ideals of interdependence, mutual care and submission, which are more fitting to members of a body.

In theory Christians are already fully committed to and responsible for one another (see, for instance, 1 John 3:16-18; John 15:12-13; 2 Cor. 8:13-15). However, since this is rarely practiced, it won't work for Christians to unilaterally commit themselves to the church universal by vowing to love and care for all Christians. This commitment needs to be particularized to a group of Christians who are willing to make the same commitment. Unless these commitments are mutual there can be no communal relationship, just as there can be no marriage without the mutual commitment of a man and a woman.

When Christians share their lives and commit themselves to one another, sacrifices are necessary. Often they need to set aside preferences about where they live for the sake of residing close enough to their brothers and sisters. Sometimes Christians in communities need to bypass promotions, or other career or educational opportunities, for the sake of the family relationship with other Christians they have committed themselves to.

When Christians are in a community relationship with one another, their relationships with one another can be second only to their commitment to the Lord Himself. And this, after all, is how it should be.

CHAPTER SIXTEEN

Mere Christian Community

by Stephen B. Clark

People have a variety of notions of Christian community. Some people picture Christian community as 20 or 30 people living together in a large house or on a farm. Other people consider Christian community to be a group of Christians who pool their finances, putting their checkbooks and bank accounts into a common pot. Others think of community as a monastic institution or religious order.

But to be a Christian community, a group of people do not have to live in one building or handle all their money in a centralized way. These are possible *forms* of Christian community. They may be good for some Christians and inappropriate for others. Fundamentally, Christian community has to do with the way Christians relate to one another. The Scriptures regard a community relationship of love, commitment and interdependence among Christians as normative, not optional.

I would like to examine three terms in the New Testament that communicate some of the scriptural vision of Christians' relationships with each other. These are terms used to describe Christians: the word *brother*; the word *koinonia*, usually translated "fellowship"; and the phrase the *body of Christ*.

Brothers and Sisters

The most common term for Christians in the New Testament is *brothers*. We might translate this "brothers and sisters in the Lord." *Brothers* was the term Christians used to refer to each other.

The love Christians are to have for each other flows from this relationship and bears its special mark. "Having purified your souls by your obedience to the truth for a sincere love of the brethren, love one another earnestly from the heart" (1 Peter 1:22). "Let brotherly love continue," we read in Hebrews 13:1. A particular Greek word, *philadelphia*, is used in such places to mean "brotherly love."

Scripture is talking about a special kind of love that exists among us because we are brothers and sisters in the Lord. But in our own culture and language we have lost much of the underlying scriptural concept of brothers and sisters. On the one hand, the words *brother* and *sister* refer to children of the same parents. On the other hand, the words are used to refer to some vague kinship among all men, as in the slogan "the brotherhood of man and the fatherhood of God."

Scripture, of course, uses *brother* and *sister* to refer to children of the same parents. However, Scripture never uses the term *brother* to refer to all mankind. It consistently uses *brother* precisely to describe situations in which there is a definite relationship among a group of people. In the New Testament, this relationship is the brotherhood of Christians; we are brothers and sisters because we are joined to one another in Christ. Non-Christians are "outsiders." For example, Paul writes, "Conduct yourselves wisely toward outsiders, making the most of the time" (Col. 4:5).

Scripture teaches that we should love and serve all men. "Love your enemies and pray for those who persecute you, so that you may be sons of your Father who is in heaven; for he makes his sun rise on the evil and on the good, and sends rain on the just and on the unjust" (Matt. 5:44-45). We are to love our enemies because God loves them and because God wants Christians to be like Him. But we are not told to love them because they are our brothers.

The early Christians understood that their faith gave them a distinctive identity which they shared with all other Christians. They saw their relationship as Christians as a relationship among members of a family; they were "born of God" (John 1:13)—born of the same Father; they were "born of the Spirit" (John 3:8)—the same spiritual blood flowed in them.

Everything was affected by the early Christians' unity in Christ. Oneness with brothers and sisters in the Lord was more important than relationships with fellow countrymen, with members of the same social class, with political allies, even with members of the same family. This was the meaning of the rebuke Jesus spoke when informed that His blood relatives had come to visit Him (Matt. 12:48-50).

The early Christians recognized one another as brothers and sisters in the Lord. Before then, the Jews also had understood themselves as brothers. Among the

Jews, *brother* meant not only "blood brother." It also meant the relationship all Jews had with one another because they were members of the Jewish people.

Jewish law spelled out the responsibilities of this relationship in some detail. Deuteronomy instructs the Jews: "At the end of every seven years...every creditor shall release what he has lent to...his brother, because the Lord's release has been proclaimed. Of a foreigner you may exact it; but whatever of yours is with your brother your hand shall release.

"You shall not harden your heart or shut your hand against your poor brother, but you shall open your hand to him, and lend him sufficient for his need, whatever it may be.

"You shall not lend upon interest to your brother.... To a foreigner you may lend upon interest, but to your brother you shall not lend upon interest; that the Lord your God may bless you in all that you undertake" (Deut. 15:1-3, 7-8; 23:19-20).

The Jews of the Old Covenant understood that their relationship with each other was different from their relationship with all men. Their relationship as brothers and sisters was a relationship of full commitment. To be members of the same people meant that each person was responsible for the welfare of all others. (See also Lev. 19:18.)

The relationship was the same for the early Christians, and it should be the same among Christians today. But today, few of us experience a definite relationship with many other Christians. We may be close to a few Christians, but most are complete strangers to us, even those who attend and support the same church.

While the early Christians made a total commitment

to each other, our commitments are increasingly fragmented and limited. When another Christian gets into trouble or incurs a need, we expect him to seek help from friends, family or a social welfare agency.

Recently, I asked myself a simple question: What would I have done if I had gotten into financial difficulty a few years ago, before the community I belong to began to understand what it means to be brothers and sisters? If I had a medical bill of several thousand dollars that I absolutely had to pay, and I had no money in the bank, to whom would I have turned? I could not have asked other members of my local church for the money. Probably they would have told me of a bank where I might get a loan, or of a welfare office where I could get public assistance. As for the men I was working with to spread the gospel, we simply did not have that kind of commitment to each other. The person I would have gone to with my need was my blood brother. Our relationship meant that I could go to him for every need in my life. I could not think of a single Christian I could have turned to for help.

Some Christians know other Christians who would help them in trouble like that. But probably these are close friends who simply happen to be Christians. But our love for other Christians should not be limited to those whom we like and can get to know personally. Brotherhood in Jesus Christ, not friendship or personal intimacy, was the basis of the brotherly love spoken of in the New Testament. The early Christian communities—and such are the communities the church needs today—encompassed all Christians in a particular area. Brotherly care means a total commitment to those who share our rebirth in Jesus Christ, even to people whom we may not know at all.

Most Christians today make limited commitments to other Christians. They can be counted on for a number of carefully specified activities. The remaining parts of their lives are private. Our commitments as Christians are usually no different from our other commitments, such as our jobs.

For many of us, the only exception to limited commitments is our family. A father makes a full commitment to his wife and children. He is responsible for the things the family does together and the things its members do alone—for his children while they are at school, for his wife while she works outside the home.

The Christian community is meant to be like a properly functioning family. The commitment of all of its members is full, encompassing all aspects of each person's life. Brothers and sisters place no limits on their responsibility for each other. We can live out this commitment because Jesus has changed us. As Christians we can say, "You are my brother," because the power that unites us is stronger and more important than anything else. The same Holy Spirit has poured the same love into our hearts.

Koinonia

The New Testament often uses a second term to describe the body of Christians, *koinonia*. The common English translation is "fellowship." "Fellowship" is not a very helpful translation because it has the connotation of a loose collection of friends. *Koinonia* means holding things in common; an exact translation would be "community." The Christians had a community; they were a group of people who shared.

The first thing they shared was the Holy Spirit. Paul

refers to the "fellowship of the Holy Spirit" or the "community of the Holy Spirit" (2 Cor. 13:14). The Spirit was the basis of the Christians' common life.

But the early Christians shared much more. They had their whole lives in common. Perhaps the best definition of Christian community is found in the Acts of the Apostles: "Now the company of those who believed were of one heart and soul, and no one said that any of the things which he possessed was his own, but they had everything in common. There was not a needy person among them, for as many as were possessors of lands or houses sold them, and brought the proceeds of what was sold and laid it at the apostles' feet; and distribution was made to each as any had need" (4:32,34,35).

Having everything in common meant that no one thought anything he possessed was his own. Everything was at the disposal of the community for the common good. Christian community, *koinonia*, means that our whole lives are in common. Our possessions, our lives, belong first to the Lord and then to our brothers and sisters in the Lord, the body of Christ. In Christian community, what's yours is mine and what's mine is yours. We do not keep parts of our lives for ourselves, unavailable to our brothers' claim on them.

The place to begin sharing, of course, is in our spiritual lives. Ironically, sometimes Christians are more likely to make great financial sacrifice to help each other than they are to talk about their prayer life, their experience of God or their love for the Lord. Our spiritual lives are the most important things we have in common. Our life with God is the reason we share a life together in community. At the beginning it is hard for many people to open up their inner lives like this, but such sharing is essential for spiritual growth; it is also the basis for other aspects of our common life.

Having our lives in common also means sharing other personal aspects of our lives. In our culture, if we sin, if we are plagued by sexual temptations, if we are anxious or depressed, we keep these problems to ourselves. Victories over our difficulties are similarly private. We might share our personal lives with our spouse or a very close friend. But most of us grow up with the firm conviction, perhaps arising from bitter experience, that our personal lives are strictly private.

However, as brothers and sisters in Christian community, nothing in our lives is entirely our own. My life belongs to my brother. I cannot construct elaborate strategies to keep him from finding out what I am really like. In fact, opening up our lives to our brothers and sisters in the Lord is usually necessary to begin overcoming our problems and experiencing the freedom that the Lord wants us to have.

Most people who belong to Christian communities where personal sharing is encouraged find quickly that they can be more free about their personal lives than they ever imagined. Personal sharing must be done with discretion and in the appropriate circumstances. But it should be done, for it is part of sharing our lives in Christian community.

Quite often, the real test of our commitment to our brothers and sisters in Christian community lies in our willingness to give up time and money. Time and money are not among the things we can keep while we give them away. We can talk about our spiritual life and still hang onto it. If we share about a victory over a personal problem, the victory is still ours. However, if our money goes to our brother's purpose, we cannot spend it on our own purpose. If we give up our time to our brothers and sisters, we cannot use it for ourselves.

When we read in Scripture about taking up the cross and laying down our lives, we can ask ourselves if these words have affected the way we make decisions about time and money. This is where we have to love as Jesus did, who gave up His life for love of men.

Scripture makes an explicit connection between the gospel and our use of material goods. "By this we know love, that he laid down his life for us; and we ought to lay down our lives for the brethren. But if any one has the world's goods and sees his brother in need, yet closes his heart against him, how does God's love abide in him? Little children, let us not love in word or speech but in deed and in truth" (1 John 3:16-18).

Our love for each other does not consist of words—even honest, holy, spiritual words. It is something that gets expressed in material terms. It is practical, concrete and sometimes painful.

This does not mean that we can produce Christian community by giving away all our money to needy Christians. A relationship with one another as brothers and sisters must come first. When that is established, then there should be *koinonia*, community, among those brothers and sisters. Many Christian groups have found themselves in serious difficulties because they have started by developing community in material terms.

The phrase the *body of Christ* is found in the letters of Paul. In Ephesians, one of his later letters, he uses the term to refer to the universal church. However, in his earlier letters he applies the term to a local

Christian assembly. He tells the Christians in Corinth that they should function as a body because they are the body of Christ. "Just as the [human] body is one and has many members, and all the members of the body, though many, are one body, so it is with Christ" (1 Cor. 12:12).

The members of the Christian body have different gifts, but they are to function in unity. "Now you are the body of Christ and individually members of it. And God has appointed in the church first apostles, second prophets, third teachers, then workers of miracles, then healers, helpers, administrators, speakers in various kinds of tongues. Are all teachers? Do all possess gifts of healing? Do all speak with tongues? Do all interpret?" (1 Cor. 12:27-30).

Being the body of Christ means much more than running orderly worship services or establishing proper procedures to make decisions and resolve disputes. It is a daily, living relationship that embraces our whole lives. We are members of the same body all the time. The relationship goes beyond the things we do in common. On the job, alone in a secular environment, we are still parts of the body of Christ. Together, we are Jesus in the world today because we are members of His body. Through us, His body, He proclaims the good news of salvation; He heals, feeds, teaches and confronts men with the truth about God.

An important implication for the church, and for all of us as individuals, is that we must begin to give up our hard-won independence and become interdependent; we must become people who depend on each other. This does not mean becoming weak or less capable of doing things. We become interdependent in order to become stronger—to do even greater things than Jesus did.

Interdependence sounds nice. However, it is much easier to acknowledge our interdependence than it is to act as though our very lives hinge on others. We experience this as difficult largely because in our culture, growing to maturity means cutting the ties that bind us to others. We learn to make our own decisions and chart our own course. Acting as a member of an interdependent body involves unlearning the habits of a lifetime.

God's plan for our maturity is not individualistic. The only complete Christian is the body of Christ. Jesus is the only individual who is complete in Himself. Today He is present in the world in the body of believers. Only the body can be whole. Anyone who wants to be a complete Christian must realize that he is part of a body, dependent on others, and must begin to act accordingly.

The interdependence and total commitment of Christians to one another is not possible without authority and submission. To be unified, a Christian body must have recognized headship. To function as a body Christians must make themselves subordinate to one another. When we put our lives and resources in common, we need to establish some person or group to take responsibility for the common life to see that it functions in good order. When Christians love one another and are one in the Lord, authority takes on the character of service. It changes from something fearful into a personal relationship we can trust.

Sometimes Christians use the term Christian community vaguely to refer to any group in which everyone is a Christian. In reality, Christian community is Christians who have a brotherly commitment to one another, who share their lives, and who live interdependently as members of a body. People working for church renewal, who want to know what Christian community is and how to build it, should begin by studying the depth of the relationship among Christians that the Scriptures envision.

CHAPTER SEVENTEEN

Building Christian Community

An Interview With Ralph C. Martin

Pastoral Renewal: Ralph, please describe what you mean when you talk about Christian community.

Ralph Martin: It can be described as a family relationship. Coming into community means passing from relationships based primarily on my convenience or my need, to relationships that are based on commitment: whether it's convenient or not, whether I need you or not, I commit myself to be a brother or sister to you.

Entering community life involves a conversion from being concerned primarily about my good and the good of my family to taking a concern for our good, the good of the people of God, the good of the body of Christ in our area. We pass from a position of independence and isolation into a relationship of interdependence into a shared life.

Living together under one roof or putting our salaries and material possessions in common is not an essential aspect of community life. The relationship of brotherhood and sisterhood with each other is essential. It can be expressed in a variety of ways.

PR: You see community as something more than what goes on in an active congregation or prayer group?

RM: There are degrees of community. Some parishes and prayer groups have elements of real community life and sharing.

But usually what's going on in a church or prayer group is a number of activities. People's relationships and commitments to one another are limited to activities together. People are not committed to caring for each other's whole lives. In most congregations and prayer groups people are pretty much alone in bearing their responsibilities and making the decisions that govern their lives.

For example, even in an active congregation or Christian group, many important questions are viewed as strictly private: whether a person takes a job promotion that would take him away to another city, when he goes on vacation, whether he moves to a new house. Decisions are made without any reference to brothers and sisters.

But in a community, where people have their whole lives in common, these choices are no longer private. They affect the local body of brothers and sisters; the outcome alters the group's ability to be a servant people. In a community, a person would take counsel about these kinds of questions, normally, by consulting his immediate pastoral leader or elder.

PR: If Christians are interested in entering a community-type relationship with one another, how can they determine if they are ready?

RM: There needs to be enough balance, stability and Christian maturity in the group to handle the deeper commitment that community life involves. If the people are new to the Christian life, if they're having problems just getting their basic responsibilities fulfilled, it's probably premature for them to think about taking on further commitments.

A more important ingredient is leadership. There must be some people who are able to serve as the heads of the community, who can take pastoral responsibility for the functioning of the whole group and for the lives of individual members. Community leadership requires people who not only have Christian maturity and stable character, but who have a high level of commitment to care for people in a pastoral way.

The potential leaders have to be able to teach—not necessarily in stupendous formal teachings, but they must be able to teach people about living the Christian life and relating to one another. They have to have some ability to discern what is happening in a situation and take appropriate action, to be patient yet firm, to gain the respect and confidence of the other people.

I don't want to make the criteria for successful leadership seem impossible. But when Scripture describes the characteristics that are needed in a person who is a pastoral leader of a community, the list is fairly impressive. In a new community, these characteristics and gifts are not going to be present in the leaders in fullblown form. But the basic ingredients would have to be there in some of the men in the group before I would encourage the group to move toward fully shared community life.

PR: What if members of a group disagree about

moving toward community?

RM: After sufficient talk, reflection and prayer with the whole group, those who want to move toward community ought to be able to go ahead, maintaining ties of brotherhood with those who don't. If people want to live in community, but live in situations where it isn't possible to build a community, they should consider moving to places where community has gotten established.

PR: What changes in the group need to be made as Christians move into community?

RM: The situation would vary somewhat from place to place, but in my experience, some structural elements need to come into being.

The first thing is that the community needs to have a way to develop its identity. For most groups this means starting a community meeting. The community I belong to grew out of a large public prayer meeting. An important step toward community was the decision to have an additional weekly meeting for those who were interested in a more committed relationship with one another. Once a community got started, some sort of community meeting becomes essential.

Second, there has to be some clarity about who is part of the community and who isn't. Community life involves a definite commitment to relate to one another in a brotherly way all the time, not just when it's convenient or when we need to. It means that we offer ourselves with our brothers and sisters to God, so that He can make us into something together. Membership in community is a very definite thing. Either a person is taking his place in the body or he isn't.

Third, in order for people to decide whether to join

the community, it must be clear what responsibilities are involved. Some groups draw up a "covenant" that spells out the commitment community members make. In the covenant, the group simply tries to express what it means to be part of the community.

A fourth element of community is some way of teaching new people about life in the Lord and in the community, and preparing them to live it.

This process of initiation has several steps. Many groups offer some basic evangelism and teaching that help people come into a new or deeper relationship with God. Afterward, people are provided an opportunity to find out more about the community itself, perhaps through a special weekend. Then people are given an opportunity to make a preliminary commitment to the community.

The fifth element should be clear from what I've said already: pastoral leadership is important. If a community does not have leaders who are clearly recognized and supported by the group, the community will find it very difficult to make any progress.

A sixth element is smaller pastoral groupings. There are various ways people can gather together in smaller groups, sharing their lives in more depth than is possible in the community as a whole, especially as the community grows in size.

Finally, regular, ongoing teaching needs to be provided to help the community's members grow in maturity and become of one mind and heart. This can be provided in courses, at the community's gatherings, and in other ways.

I hope I'm not presenting a picture of community as something that is impossibly hard to do. It is difficult.

It's challenging. It takes a growing degree of maturity and commitment and patience. But it's also something the Holy Spirit does with us and through us. We experienced the growth of our community as God's mercy on us. A lot of what happened has not been our wisdom but the mercy of God and the love of God.

PR: What advice would you give leaders of a group that is becoming a community?

RM: First, I would advise people moving toward community to get in touch with some established community, learn from their mistakes, and get the help and guidance they need. Second, a newly emerging community can become fixated on some particular project, like starting a school or overcoming social problems, before it is anywhere near ready. In some countries there can be a preoccupation with national problems; people may prematurely offer their community as a solution to these great problems. This lack of realism is often fatal to the community's development.

I believe it is overwhelmingly important that the leaders be in the proper relationship with one another. If the leaders learn to love and be patient with one another, to trust and work with one another, to submit to one another in the right way, then a lot of problems other people face as they move toward community can be worked through.

A very important decision at the start of our community's development was the commitment that a few leaders made to one another. We agreed to work together no matter what the difficulties, and to offer ourselves together to the Lord for Him to build something with us. I think that was the basis for everything that God did later in forming us into a community. The commitment we made was extended to other potential leaders in the group. This group then constituted a core of people who could help one another begin to care for the life of the community.

The leaders also need to have a pastoral concern for one another. One of the greatest problems in the church today is: who pastors the pastors? It is helpful to have some of the older leaders take a pastoral responsibility for the younger ones. Even where the leaders' group is made up of people of equal maturity and experience, it's good to set up pastoring relationships within the whole body of leaders so that all get cared for.

PR: Do you think a community should let everyone join who agrees to the required commitment, or should the community exercise control over who enters it?

RM: There's a tendency for people with serious problems to be drawn to a group of loving Christians. But a community can never develop to the point where it can undertake long-range, sustained service if it takes on more than its members can properly handle at the beginning. This prevents the group from establishing the basic relationships and pattern of life together that would put them in a better position to help people with serious problems.

Time put into developing the community isn't time taken away from serving the Lord. I think that in the beginning most communities can take everybody who might be willing to join. They ought to take as many people as can be properly cared for, who have a reasonable stability and maturity, and very few, if any, people who have serious problems.

Another situation calls for careful examination: often wives want to join but their husbands don't. The leaders need to be sure these women don't become involved in community in a way that shifts their center of gravity away from their role in the family.

Many communities have adopted a policy of not receiving women into a full commitment with the community without their husbands. These groups feel it would be almost impossible for a wife to be faithful to both her family commitment and community commitment unless her husband is involved. Other communities, while not ruling out the possibility of a wife becoming a member without her husband, are very concerned to see that her community involvement makes her more loving and effective at home.

PR: What would you say to people who conclude that their group is not in the position to form community?

RM: If the basic elements for community-building don't yet exist in a group, some meaningful steps can be taken.

For example, people could begin to come together in an informal way, to share some meals, or to have some family outings and activities together—things that help people open up their lives and get to know each other more. Or they could get together for explicitly spiritual purposes, talking about their lives with one another in depth, praying for special things.

They could help each other—loaning lawn mowers, painting each other's houses—showing love and concern in ways that go beyond a weekly meeting.

PR: Is there anything you would like to say in conclusion?

RM: In the future it's going to be very difficult for Christians to persevere and flourish without the support of brothers and sisters in some kind of community life.

It's going to be very difficult to maintain a steady Christian witness and carry on the mission of Christ with power and grace except in the context of Christian community. I think that the anti-Christian pressure in society is mounting. The pressure in schools and universities, in the media and entertainment, is making it more and more difficult for people to sustain a confident, joyful Christian life outside some kind of community. I am convinced that in the years ahead community is going to be seen not merely as an option for Christians, but as something at the heart of the gospel and essential to Christian life.

Part VI

PUTTING IT ALL TOGETHER: FOUR CASE STUDIES

Reading about pastoral concepts is one thing. Seeing them operate in practice is another. This section presents case studies of four groups that have structured their life and pastoral care around the principles outlined in this book.

Churches and communities are living organisms, and like all living things they grow and change over time. The groups described here will have grown and changed in many ways since these descriptions were written, though all of them are still very much alive and still operating according to the same basic patterns.

CHAPTER EIGHTEEN

Gulf Coast Fellowship

by Kevin Perrotta

Terry Parker is a pastor with clean hands. He is sitting across a table from Bill McLaughlin, a younger man who has looked to Terry for pastoral guidance for the last ten years. The two men are discussing Bill's transition from the sixties' counterculture to full-time lay ministry and youth work. Terry talks softly, chews mints and from time to time folds and unfolds his hands.

They are clean, without a trace of grease. Meeting him for the first time, one might be surprised to learn that Terry entered pastoral work not from a seminary but from a service station, which he ran for many years before he started to take a pastoral concern for other men in the church.

Gerry VanIwaarden is describing how he cares for some younger men in the church. There is Ralph, for example. Ralph's job is low-paying and otherwise unrewarding. Gerry has been helping him identify his gifts and choose a new direction.

In the meantime, Gerry is helping Ralph take advantage of an opportunity in his current job. Ralph has to supervise several people. This means learning to give directions, to stand up to people, to say no. It's a maturing experience for Ralph.

Gerry himself went through a job change last year. Climbing interest rates depressed the construction industry and put him out of business as a contractor. Now he works for another construction company—outdoors, one gathers, from his deeply tanned face and arms.

Where womanly friendship ends and pastoral care begins is, from Kathy Stanko's description, a little hard to say. A red-haired woman in her early thirties, she leans forward and describes the help she gives some younger married women. Training them in family relationships is a part of it. There is working together in each other's homes, and some counseling.

A good portion of the relationship is setting an example. Kathy expands on this element by expressing how she herself has been helped by other women she has looked to in the church. Of one woman she says, "When I see her, I want to be like her. I feel inspired to be like her in the way she lives as a Christian and loves her family. What's helpful is having other people around that you see and know, who love the Lord, and having access to their lives."

These people are members of Gulf Coast Covenant Church, in Mobile, Alabama. One of them, Terry Parker, is an ordained elder of the church. Like some of the other 20-or-so elders, he became a full-time pastor in mid-life, after growing into the role through practical experience. Gerry VanIwaarden and Kathy Stanko are typical of the many men and women in the church who give some pastoral care to other members while continuing in secular occupations and domestic responsibilities.

The members of Gulf Coast Church believe that any church's ability to carry out its mission is no stronger than the people and relationships within it. As the church's senior pastor, Charles Simpson, puts it, a church's success in any sphere must be based on "what it is doing in the individual's life."

So the leaders of Gulf Coast have organized the church in ways that aim at bringing individual members to maturity as Christians. That means involving many members in giving practical training and pastoral care. Actually, it means involving every member of the church.

A Pastoral Network

The 1100-member church is divided into house churches of six to eight families plus singles. Each group has a leader who is in turn receiving pastoral care. In the first group the leader is learning to take a pastoral concern for the members of the group. In the second relationship he receives training and care himself.

A quick bit of arithmetic will show that this arrangement draws a large number of people into pastoral service. It also positions pastoral care at the level of daily life. The leader and everyone in the house church can get to know one another well.

John Stanko, Kathy's husband, explains how he leads a group of nine families. Among his goals for the men in the group—eight of whom have married fairly recently—are to lead them into serving each other and to help them get established in their careers. Right now both purposes are furthered by getting the men together often for work on Saturdays.

One man in the group has started a landscaping business, another a construction outfit. Opportunities for contracts that would build up their businesses come their way, but would require hiring more employees than they can really afford. John and the other men in the group help by putting in some time together to get the jobs done. The proceeds that would have gone for wages go to whichever men in the group particularly need some financial help.

John explains that working together provides an opportunity to help the men grow in good work habits and relationships. "I can see if the men are diligent, if they're attentive to detail, whether they come across badly in work relationships." If he sees weaknesses, he points them out and shows the men how to change.

John also finds recreation together an important opportunity for pastoring. The church has its own softball league in the city's recreational sports system. The men in John's group all play. "You get to see how a man reacts when he's angry. Does the bat go over the fence? Does he argue with the umpire? How does he handle it when he thinks he should be playing rather than someone else?"

Of course, the softball diamond offers a lot of good examples, too. John admits that controlling anger has been a challenge for him. "I can look at brothers out there," John says, "who are strong but have their strength under control. That's an inspiration."

The house churches are more than pastoral units. They are a way of fostering relationships as brothers and sisters in Christ. "I find that I'm spending more time together with the people in the group,'' John observes, ''less of it specifically pastoral as time goes by.''

Once settled in a group, members usually stay put. This gives people a chance to put down roots in their relationships. David Holcomb, a young realtor, remarks that one of the most important changes for him since he joined Gulf Coast Church about three years ago is knowing that he now has relationships which will last.

''Before, in the fraternity or the navy, I had good friends. But as soon as you knew someone was going to be leaving town, things cooled off. Here I have the sense of really being brothers. On Saturday some of us helped a man in our group move. I had other work I wanted to do here at home, but it was good to work hard and come home exhausted at the end of the day, knowing that we had worked together as brothers and have an enduring relationship with each other.''

David's wife, Susan, explains in an enthusiastic voice that the women in their group have found an equal degree of satisfaction in their relationships. ''Through the week we will help each other with caring for children—our children are similar ages and most of us live within a couple of miles of each other. Sometimes we will help each other with cleaning, especially if someone will be entertaining. We'll get together to do crewel or needlepoint. Whatever we are doing, we enjoy having the time to be together and visit with each other.

The small groups meet weekly, in addition to the various informal contacts, work and recreation that the members have together. The weekly meetings are seen as a family time, a time to draw everyone together for prayer, sharing and relaxation.

David and Susan cite family life as their key area of

change since they have become members of the church. David is articulate about what has made a difference. "Being part of the church has given us clear standards about how to relate as a husband and wife, how to raise our children. I had been irresponsible in some ways at home. I began taking more responsibility and initiative. Things with the children changed as we took a more consistent approach to discipline."

Previously David and Susan had been thinking she would go to work when their three children were all in school. "David was looking forward to the time when I would do something useful," Susan remarks with a twinkle. Now they have decided that for them her work at home is more important than an outside job, and she is planning to continue at home full time.

Many churches today are experimenting with principles that operate in Gulf Coast Covenant Church, such as small groups, lay involvement in pastoral care, and education by real-life example rather than in a classroom. Gulf Coast has carried these principles farther and deeper than most other churches. A look at its history helps explain why this is so.

Gulf Coast Covenant Church began in 1972. Its origins, however, go back at least ten years earlier to the pastoral experience of a handful of people, including two Southern Baptist pastors, Charles Simpson and John Duke.

Charles launched into pastoral work with a vengeance at age 20. He was invited to pastor a congregation of about 80 members. "I was what you might call a rebel with a cause," he says. "I was a tremendous visitor; I visited all of our membership every two months. I had the idea that the church was full of committed, sincere people who really wanted Jesus Christ made known on the earth. But I couldn't get participation. If there were 80 members, only 40 would be in church on Sunday. But somehow the other 40 felt free to call themselves Christians."

By what Charles terms "sheer zeal" the congregation grew to about 300 members. A measure of the strain he put himself under is that at age 26 he was hospitalized with the symptoms of a heart attack. "The doctor told me I was under tremendous stress and that I needed to give up something."

Charles found himself frustrated. "There seemed to me to be only two options. Either the church was once what the book of Acts said it was, in which case we were subnormal by a long shot. Or it never was what Acts said, and then I really had nothing to preach."

John Duke, meanwhile, was pastoring a church in Mississippi. "We were doing pretty well in terms of numbers," says John, a bearded man who listens carefully and responds quickly in conversation. "We were having—for a little rural church—quite a large number of people baptized. But many of them would not last much more than six months to a year.

"I was disturbed that there didn't seem to be a consistency, a joy, in the lives of many of our people. They were up one day, down the next. I felt we lacked the dynamic to maintain the life that people had come to know."

A series of events moved Charles and John some steps closer to their pastoral goals. Charles had an experience which "could be referred to in a number of ways, but was an overwhelming experience with the Holy Spirit." Things began to happen in the church which he had not been able to accomplish.

"We had people coming forward to pray before I gave the altar call. People began to come and want to pray at other times, so I set aside Saturdays for prayer. There was a season of revival in the church. We broke all records for attendance, conversions and financial giving, right in the middle of the summer.

"Things happened for people. One lady, who was a department store executive, had tried to take her life. She was on alcohol and was in the psychiatric ward of a hospital. I didn't try to explain anything to her. I just went to visit her, held her hand and prayed for her. And she was healed—spiritually, mentally, physically. That sort of thing happened."

Charles and John met. Soon afterward John also had a deeper encounter with the Holy Spirit. A few months later he left his church in Mississippi and joined Charles as associate pastor in Mobile.

A fresh experience of the Holy Spirit turned out to be necessary but not enough. People's degree of dedication to the Lord rose. They knew God's love more deeply. "But what happened then," Charles explains, "was that I began to see that the church was not really able to give personal care. A lot of things are not in the category of needing a miracle. They are in the category of needing personal attention. A miracle won't take the place of lack of wisdom over a period of time.

"For instance, one man was converted who had a background of working for a circus. There was no stability in his life. He was a zealous man, but after a short period of time he fancied himself to be a prophet. People like this had to be told that before you can be a prophet you must first become a stable person. You've got to develop what I would call just practical sense."

The pastors were shocked to discover that among the many non-members who were coming regularly, two couples divorced and one husband married the other wife—without the pastors knowing it had happened.

"I felt pastorally that I was failing," Charles explains. "I was creating more dynamic than I could channel. I saw a terrific pastoral need. So I began to try to enlist the traditional Christians—those who had a good background and knew a lot of Scripture—into giving personal care to new people. I found it a very difficult thing to accomplish."

The very success of Charles, John and others brought to head a still unremedied deficiency in the church. "The whole church wants pastoral care, but only a small minority actually becomes involved in giving it. People don't think of themselves as parts of the body of Christ. Not everyone's called to be a pastor. But we're all called to care for one another."

Given this mixture of success and frustration, Charles and John both left the congregation for teaching and traveling.

Two years later Gulf Coast Covenant Church began to take shape, along different lines. A couple of years' reflection had led Charles, John and two other friends (one of them Terry Parker; the other Glen Roachelle, who now pastors in Dallas) to see the practical importance of personal training for reaching maturity in Christian living. They saw the model of this kind of training in Jesus' relationship with the twelve. They also saw it in certain kinds of secular training—in the way a musician tutors a student or a craftsman instructs an apprentice.

And they saw the principle in their own lives. John recognized he had originally joined Charles not only to serve the church but to learn from him. All four men found they had a few pastoral relationships with people who had come to them over the years seeking more than advice. There were a few who came looking for training as well as counsel, correction as well as encouragement. These were relationships where they saw they had been particularly effective.

"I could see that I had been discipled by my father," Charles says. "I could see that almost every minister relates to at least a few people this way, whether he is aware of it or not. But I realized you can do it better if you know what you're doing."

As the four men understood it, the relationship had several characteristics. It meant that a person let the pastor get to know him thoroughly and invited him to have input into any department of his life. It meant a personal relationship—a sense of commitment to love and serve one another. People would enter the relationship because they were looking for training and felt that the other person set a good example of Christian living. The goal was to bring the person to a greater ability to handle his responsibilities and serve God. The training aspect of the relationship would pass away in time, leaving a relationship of pastoral concern and lasting friendship.

Gulf Coast Covenant Church began as the four men brought together 80 people who wanted this kind of relationship. In the past eight years, many of these 80 have taken on pastoral care for new people who have come. Some of these, in turn, have reached the point of caring for others.

For the original group, the training nature of the relationship has largely given way to ongoing pastoral care and friendship. For the newer people, such as David and Susan Holcomb, there is an experience of training in Christian family life, qualities of Christian character, and so on.

Charles, John and the other early leaders admit they have made mistakes along the way. But they find that their current approach better answers the pastoral needs they see than the other models they worked with.

Charles points to Terry Parker as an example. Terry was a gas station operator who belonged to the Baptist church Charles pastored. "Terry never exactly came to me and asked to be trained," Charles says. "What happened was that he said, 'Come over to my house. My wife and I want to talk with you.' After that visit he would say, 'When can you come back?' I found myself gravitating to him. I felt directed to give input, and after a period of time I saw that the things I said to him and his wife had far greater impact than what I said normally to most people. His questions all reflected this concern, 'How can you help me do the will of God?' "

Charles describes similar relationships that formed spontaneously before Gulf Coast Church started, and more deliberately afterward. "Many of these people are full-time pastors today. Virtually all of them are involved intensely in the Lord's service. So I feel the mortality rate for infant Christians is much lower with this kind of approach than the kind of birth that takes place without personal care and training."

The result is a Christian life-style in the church that is noticeable to the visitor and attracts some attention in the city of Mobile. For instance, Gulf Coast's members treat each other with a graciousness and generosity that might be seen as a Christian enlargement of some of the finer aspects of Southern culture.

In John Duke's office, for example, one wall is filled with bookshelves built for him as a gift by two members of the church. The Stankos' yard ranks in the *Better Homes and Gardens* class, due to the kindness of the landscape contractor in their house church. When one woman's husband died last year, the leader of their small group and his wife accompanied her to Boston at their own expense for the funeral.

One notices the church's members' loyalty to one another in the ways they speak about each other. In a four-day visit, I heard not a word of criticism of another member, and a lot of praise of other members' good qualities and gifts. There was no unwillingness to discuss problems or weaknesses in the church's life, only an unwillingness to discuss each others' problems and weaknesses.

In Mobile the church is widely known. It is one of the largest in town and has an unusual structure. It has other characteristics that make it unusual. The social-class spread is somewhat broader than that of most predominantly middle-class churches, containing a larger proportion of folks at the poorer end of the spectrum. Also one of the church's leaders who takes one of the most prominent public roles in the church and the city is a black man, Joseph Garlington. Gulf Coast is not the only interracial congregation in Mobile, but it is one of only a few. Joseph's prominence, and the fact that he has more whites than blacks under his care, is more significant in Deep-South Mobile than it might be in some other cities.

Why It Works

Why has Gulf Coast Covenant Church been successful in building a strong church life using principles such as small group relationships and lay pastoral care? A long list of reasons might be compiled. Five that are especially important are:

1. A spiritual approach. The leaders of Gulf Coast Covenant Church have sought not only to learn principles but to follow the guidance of the Holy Spirit. They do not claim perfection in this. But they believe that Christian leadership involves seeking the Spirit's leading. For the leaders of Gulf Coast Church, this does not mean mastering spiritual techniques. Basically, it involves striving not to let anything become more important than God Himself and looking to one another for discernment.

At a recent elders' meeting, for example, the leaders took considerable time for discussion of the need to maintain a first love for the Lord. "Everything must be birthed out of devotion to the Lord," one said. "We mustn't substitute 'good works' for that."

Of shared discernment John Duke says, "I have found the safety involved in having to share what I believe God is saying, and having other men of God say, 'I bear witness to that,' or, 'I feel that's not altogether right.' "

A spiritual approach also means a conscious reliance on the work of the Spirit. For example, one elder says, "You can't exactly teach a man loyalty or faithfulness. You can teach a man to *understand* loyalty or faithfulness, and you can give him the example. But you can't *implant* those qualities in him. The Holy Spirit does that."

2. Commitment. The initial group of leaders made a commitment to one another before bringing others into committed relationships. They promised to honor and serve one another and open themselves to correction and discernment. John Duke remarks that only after he made this commitment was he able effectively to lead others into it.

The commitment runs deep. It is expressed in the fact that some members of the church have moved across the country to be part of the church. Gulf Coast's members have been willing to invest themselves in the church. If they had not, house churches, lay pastoral relationships and the rest would work very differently.

3. Clear goals. The goal is not to be in a training relationship but to live the manner of life of the kingdom of God. Personal pastoral care is a way to get there. As Charles Simpson describes it, it is a "natural method for growing into the righteousness and peace and joy of being under the government of Jesus Christ."

Gulf Coast Covenant Church gives extensive teaching about the practical implications of living in the kingdom. A feature of the teaching is an emphasis on covenant. As a body of Christians, the members of the church see themselves in an enduring, committed, covenantal relationship with one another in particular, and with other Christians.

This practical teaching sets a clear set of goals for pastoral work in the church. Each pastoral leader understands what qualities of loyalty, service, graciousness, honor, hospitality, faithfulness and integrity he desires to see built into the people in his care.

4. Example and access. "One of the greatest helps," Terry Parker says, "is the example you hold out before people. All that I can speak out of is what I have actually learned and mastered in my own life—what I have received in the Holy Spirit.

"A man picks out things that he sees in another man, and he decides, 'I want to be like that man—the way he leads his family, the way he disciplines his children, the way he plans his home.' He watches that, and then he asks questions: 'How do you do this? How do you do that?'

The simple theme of learning from the example and character of others runs like a thread throughout Gulf Coast Covenant Church. For it to work, at least three things are needed: people who are mature enough for others to imitate; people who are humble enough to learn from others; and relationships in which there is enough access to each other's everyday lives. Trust is also needed.

The unique pastoral set-up of Gulf Coast Covenant Church is not a model for every church. Not every church is in a position to develop the kind of full commitment of Gulf Coast Church. But within the scope of more limited commitments, pastoral leaders can apply principles of lay leadership, small groups, teaching by example, building strong relationships and concentrating on developing Christian character. Gulf Coast Church offers an instructive example of how these principles can be put into practice. And it provides a picture of what the results might look like.

CHAPTER NINETEEN

The People of Hope

by Kevin Perrotta

To find the People of Hope, one needs a car with a tank full of gas and a map of northeastern New Jersey. To grasp what this 500-member association of Christians is all about, one needs to forego usual ideas about how a body of Christians can share their lives and carry on Christian outreach.

The variety in the members' lives and services is striking. In fact, at first it is difficult to see what the People of Hope have in common besides a willingness to spend considerable time driving the distances that lie between them.

For example, the way to Bruce and Pat Weyand's home in Harrington Park, in the far northeastern corner of the state, lies through miles of well-established, tree-shaded suburbs. Bruce, who is a leader of the People of Hope, is also a physical education teacher at a nearby high school. Among other things, he is in charge of a network of small fellowship groups for Hope people in his area.

An hour away is Patricia Brennan, a Catholic nun connected with St. Antoninus parish in Newark. St. Antoninus Church fronts on South Orange Avenue—a street of decaying buildings, less-than-prosperous businesses, and storefront churches. Around St. Antoninus are grouped a massive rectory, closed school buildings, and a partially vacant convent where Sister Brennan lives with several other women belonging to Hope. They have a spiritual outreach to the neighborhood and run a nursery school.

From Newark one may go southeast to the home of Ed and Pat Ahern at the Jersey shore. Ed has helped organize conferences sponsored by the People of Hope. And with others at the shore, the Aherns extend warm-weather hospitality to Hope members who take the Garden State Parkway from less pleasant spots in New Jersey's urban northeast. From the shore, one may go west to New Brunswick, where some women of Hope have helped steer a Catholic school into the service of inner-city children.

Indeed, one can go in any direction in northeastern Jersey, and ever east to Long Island, and find members of the People of Hope serving the Lord in some way or another.

It would not seem likely that people so different and dispersed could form a group having much cohesiveness. But, in fact, almost any member of Hope will describe how coming into contact with the fellowship and then joining it has deeply changed his or her life. For many it has been instrumental in their coming to an adult commitment to Christ. Many have been drawn into Christian service, especially evangelism, for the first time.

Despite distances, the group has an extensive sharing of life. Members see one another often and know one another well. A visitor notices an unusual level of affection and attentiveness to one another's needs among the members. They pitch in to meet the ordinary demands of life—when a family is moving or a washing machine breaks down, when a baby arrives, when someone is sick. While the group does not practice community of goods, a fair amount of sharing, loaning and giving away takes place. In a few instances members have loaned or given substantial amounts of money to make it possible for fellow members to buy homes.

And this life together has not developed at the expense of outreach. The People of Hope has put on a spiritual renewal program, called a Jesus Week, more than 275 times in Catholic parishes in the area. It has held evangelistic gatherings in public places such as Asbury Park at the Jersey shore, which have attracted hundreds of people. It has sponsored ecumenical rallies on Pentecost at several New Jersey sites, bringing together more than 100,000 people over the last five years. The list of Hope's outreaches is a long one.

At a time of weakening relationships among church members, the People of Hope demonstrates the possibility of Christians building a strong life together. The fellowship has put down roots in the unlikely soil of urban decay and suburban transience, at the center of the megalopolis stretching from Boston to Washington, D.C. Its significant, if incomplete, success in developing shared life and ministry may thus contain some lessons for pastoral leaders dealing with the profound contemporary disintegration of family life and natural community.

Small Beginnings

The association began with Jim Ferry, a Roman Catholic priest who became involved in the charismatic renewal in the late sixties. With a few other priests and nuns he started a "house of prayer," which might be described as a drop-in retreat center. The group followed a pattern of communal prayer, with celebration of the eucharist, Scripture study, personal sharing and other activities. Outsiders—clergy and lay people—were welcome to join them for periods from a few days to several months.

The house of prayer was a sort of floating revival. (The group actually moved from one location to another.) Priests, nuns and lay people flowed through and experienced conversion and spiritual renewal. Various activities flourished inside and outside the house. H.O.P.E., as it is called ("house of prayer experience"), was a point of intensive activity within the charismatic renewal that was affecting many Catholics in New Jersey.

H.O.P.E.'s evangelistic efforts brought the group into contact with hundreds of lay people, but at first there was no way for them to join. How could families move into a former convent—where H.O.P.E. was—and have a common life with a group of priests and nuns? Nevertheless, some married and single people were strongly attracted to H.O.P.E. They found it a source of teaching about how to grow in the Christian life, and they were drawn by the residents' community life.

For example, one family that gravitated to H.O.P.E. was the Gallics. Bob Gallic was a Wall Street stockbroker who had undergone a conversion to Christ that was radically reordering his priorities. In H.O.P.E. he found a group of people who were serious about living their Christianity in a total way, and in Ferry he found a man who could help him reorient his talents and energies into Christian service.

Among the residents of H.O.P.E. and lay people such as Bob and Ginny Gallic, a vision developed for a community life that would include all of them. At the center of the vision was the realization that, in the words of Sister Brennan, "to love Jesus with heart and mind and soul one needs to have the support and help of other people who want to do the same."

In May 1977 about 100 people, of whom about 10 were priests and nuns, decided to make a commitment to one another. They agreed to a covenant that involved accepting responsibility as brothers and sisters in Christ to care for each other's whole lives and to be available to God for His service not only as individuals but as a body.

The group wanted to move beyond the first stages of spiritual renewal to a transformation, as Gallic says, of "all the areas of our lives—marriages, work, relationships with others, character as men and women." H.O.P.E. became the People of Hope. The members wanted to be a people—men and women leading the Christian way of life together in a manner that affected every area of their lives.

Leadership

Several aspects of the People of Hope are particularly instructive and lead to some conclusions about principles for pastoral renewal today.

The nature of leadership plays a formative role in any

group. In Hope, the overall leadership is composed of a group of 11 men, including Ferry, Gallic and Weyand. Two of the men are priests. The others are laymen, all of whom, except for Gallic and one other man, hold ordinary full-time jobs. Lew Ferris, for example, is a pharmaceuticals salesman in New Brunswick. Jack Costanzo runs a small electronics parts distribution business from an office in his home in Berkeley Heights. The men range in age from their 30s to their 50s.

In Hope these overall leaders are called coordinators. They could be understood as the elders of the community, in the New Testament sense of the term.

While they have the final responsibility for decisions in the fellowship, they are not primarily managers, because Hope is not primarily an organization set up to carry out certain activities—as businesses, schools and, to a great extent, most churches are set up. As the leaders of a community, the coordinators' primary responsibility is pastoral in a broad sense. Their aim is that the whole community be growing in love for God, obedience to His way of life and service to Him. While this involves making decisions, the coordinators see their task mainly as leading the community in living the Christian way of life together.

Thus the criteria for leadership are not dynamic personality, great organizational skills, public speaking ability or particular educational background. Rather the criteria are maturity in living out scriptural teaching about love of God, character, relationships with other people and handling the responsibilities of one's state of life. When the coordinators and the rest of the community identify such a man, who also has shown himself able to help others live the Christian life, he may, through a process of consultation, be added to the body of coordinators.

The coordinators invest time in their relationships with one another. In addition to a weekly evening meeting to handle business matters, they come together another evening a week to develop their friendship with one another. This means prayer, talking about how their lives are going, discussing topics, and recreational activities. The coordinators also set aside times outside the weekly meeting to deepen their own and their families' relationships.

Several reasons impel the men to put such a high priority on their relationships with each other. For one thing, they believe that anyone giving pastoral care to others needs personal support and care himself. For another, they see the growth of brotherly love among themselves as necessary if all the members of the fellowship are to develop that kind of love.

The coordinators' group is thus a laboratory for a process that is essential to Hope's development—Christians making a commitment to love and serve one another, and then, on the basis of that commitment, developing friendships and a social life together.

"It takes a whole lot of sacrifice," Gallic observes, for the coordinators to build their relationships, living as they do at distances of up to an hour and a half from a common meeting place. But Gallic actually finds some advantage in this. "Making sacrifices for one another strengthens people and builds up the community."

Pastoral Structures

Several pastoral structures are vital to Hope's life. Among these are a system of geographical districts, a process of initiation, personal pastoral relationships, and small groups.

Each coordinator cares for a geographical subgrouping called a district. Hope has eight districts, with about 80 adults in each.

A district is supposed to be small enough to allow everyone in it to know everyone else. It is also intended to be small enough that everyone is drawn into active service; there should be no room for backwaters in which people drift into passivity.

On the other hand, a district is supposed to be large enough to bring together a good mix of people of different ages and talents. A certain "critical mass" is required for a district to do the things that Hope districts normally do—fortnightly charismatic meetings for worship and teaching, social events, evangelistic efforts, activities for the youngsters, and so on.

With the assistance of other men and women in the district, the coordinator works to see that the members of the district are growing in Christian maturity, love for one another and Christian service. These are goals that pastoral leaders outside the People of Hope would share, of course. Some of the reasons for Hope's success lie in the structures that accompany the district system.

The People of Hope have formulated a workable solution to an important problem faced by vibrant churches and Christian groups, namely, how to allow for numerical growth without diluting the fervor and sense of purpose that characterized the original group. The leaders of Hope have deliberately constructed a process by which men and women are brought into the life of the community. A person might enter the process at any of several points—by coming to an evangelistic breakfast, through workmates who belong to Hope, by attending a social occasion such as a picnic. These contacts are designed to lead people to activities, such as retreats and short courses, that present the gospel and help people make a commitment of themselves to Christ and open themselves to the power of the Holy Spirit.

In each district a team of people works to build friendships with new people and introduce them to others in the community. The leaders of the teams also begin to explain a little about community life to the new people. If they are interested, they are invited to a special weekend retreat that offers some experience of community and instruction about Christian self-identity, growing in relationship with God, and community life.

People may then begin a series of courses that give practical teaching about Christian living, and they are invited to make an "underway" commitment to the community. The teaching begins with topics such as how to grow in faith, what Christian love is, how to overcome temptations, and counsel about Christian child-rearing.

The process of initiation continues for a couple of years, leading to formal, "public" commitment. During this time new men and women actually live as members of the community while receiving extensive teaching from Scripture on subjects such as how to handle emotions as a Christian, what the qualities of Christian character are, sexuality and family life, the order of Hope's community life and growing as servants of God. Personal pastoral care and placement in a small group are important factors in helping the new people appropriate the teaching and be integrated into the community.

The lengthy process of initiation serves to add to the community members who share in its level of commitment and way of life. Negatively, the process allows those who do not really want to embrace Hope's ideals to see what the fellowship is all about and withdraw from the entry process. Positively, the process presents the fellowship's vision for Christian living, helps motivate new people to make the vision their own, and facilitates their forming friendships with community members. The process also introduces newcomers to the way of life that the members of the fellowship are following and helping each other follow.

The People of Hope has found that individuals can be helped by having a continuing relationship with a more mature Christian who can show how to put Christian teaching into practice, can provide encouragement to overcome obstacles and temptations, and can offer counsel based on longer experience.

The community life of Hope provides the context for these pastoral relationships. Both parties in the relationship share their lives in community at various levels, so the texture of the relationship is brotherly or sisterly rather than professional or problem-oriented. If the one being cared for is eager to learn and the other has real maturity, good judgment and insight, the relationship can help the one being cared for understand and overcome weaknesses and faults and grow in identifying and making use of gifts.

The coordinator or other person providing this kind of care might, for example, help a person put his budget into an order that reflects Christian priorities, or help a man care for his wife and children more responsibly, or help a woman get free of anxiety. The relationship of personal pastoral care works differently according to a person's state in life, the initiative they take in seeking counsel, and whether they are just coming into the fellowship or have been a member for a few years. Men and women just entering the community receive more intense pastoral care, designed to help them make the basic changes involved in conversion to Christ and entry into community.

For many members of Hope, day-to-day community life is focused in the small group they belong to. The small groups of about a half-dozen men or women form the basic pastoral units of community. A weekly meeting for prayer, encouragement and so on is standard. In addition, the members of the small group develop as much shared life as they are able, given distances.

These men's and women's groups provide each member with a small number of brothers or sisters in Christ with whom they can concretely live out the commitments that are involved in community membership. These are the men and women for whom one is especially called to lay down one's life and with whom one especially shares one's life, spiritual and material. In the last couple of years, the community has been moving to give the men's and women's groups long-term stability in order to encourage depth in the relationships.

Key Principles

While structures such as men's and women's groups and methods such as personal pastoral care have contributed to Hope's growth, several even more basic principles underlie the fellowship's success. Three of them might be summarized as: "conversion," "clear teaching" and "commitment."

Conversion stands for the manner in which Hope

brings the basic issue of conversion to Christ front and center. Many Christians today are sensing the need for a deeper life of prayer. Many pastors of Catholic parishes make room for an "evangelical emphasis" by accommodating the local charismatic renewal group or Cursillo group. But many pastoral leaders do not clearly recognize that many of the Christians in their care simply lack a committed personal relationship with Christ.

The People of Hope is notable for its clarity about the fundamental importance of personal relationship with Christ as Lord, a changed life and an ongoing experience of the Holy Spirit. The community originated as a group of people who had begun to know the thoroughly life-changing impact of conversion to Christ and openness to the Holy Spirit. The community has been a way of seeking to extend that impact into every aspect of life.

This appreciation of the importance of conversion shapes every aspect of the association's life. One consequence is that members are highly motivated to be taught and to serve. Pastoral care proceeds on the assumption that the Holy Spirit is working in individual members, rather than on leaders' abilities to pull, please, or push.

Clear teaching points to the coordinators' presentation of clear, practical instruction about matters of Christian living—what it means to be humble, how to be a good mother, how to live out a commitment to be brothers and sisters in Christ, how to be reconciled when someone has done something wrong, how to deal with anger in a positive way, and so on. When this kind of scriptural teaching is combined with pastoral assistance, people have the experience of actually knowing what Christian living is and gradually entering into it.

This contrasts with the confusion about even basic issues of Christian living which many Christians meet today in their parishes and congregations. Is fornication always wrong? What kinds of responsibilities do I have as a father and how do I carry them out? What is a Christian approach to handling my money?

The coordinators of Hope do not pretend to have the answers to every question about Christian living in the modern world, but they believe that many answers are available if Christians take Scripture seriously as a guide to living and draw on the wealth of Christian wisdom of the past and present.

One of the important results of clear teaching is that a common way of life is defined which members can support each other in living out. This does not mean that everyone parts his hair on the same side, but that, for example, everyone respects families' need to have some times each week together, and members regard daily personal prayer as a basic obligation and encourage each other in it.

Clear teaching releases pastoral care from the sort of vague exhortation into which much preaching and counseling fall. With clear ideals for character and relationships, the preaching, teaching, organizing and personal pastoral care can be better directed. And when the leaders' vision of the Christian life becomes concrete, they can better evaluate their efforts at building it up.

Commitment refers here primarily to members' relationships with one another. There has been a great deal of discussion about the best principle on which to build up a church or other Christian body. Should Christian leaders seek to build up homogeneous units—churches with people from the same socioeconomic and ethnic backgrounds? Should neighborhood parishes be fostered? Should churches be built on different interests, such as missions, social action, style of piety and so on? Should churches concentrate on ministries to "client-groups" such as teens, the aged and the divorced?

The People of Hope shows the value of building on members' recognition of their relationship as brothers and sisters in Christ. When Christians make a commitment to love and serve one another as the New Testament teaches that brothers and sisters in Christ ought to do, then the Christian body can contain people with a variety of gifts, callings, states of life, and social and ethnic backgrounds. When people voluntarily make a commitment to live out Christian brotherly commitment with a specific body of fellow Christians, they are better able to deal with stresses and difficulties in their relationships than if they have joined a particular body because of similarity of backgrounds in interests.

When men and women make a deliberate commitment to one another to live the Christian life and serve God together, there is a foundation for order, stability and strength. On the basis of brotherly and sisterly commitment, a network of relationships can be built. These relationships are neither function-oriented, as in an institutional setting, nor are they shifting and unstable, as many friendships and interest groups are. Rather, the relationships have family qualities—they are enduring, personal, concerned with every aspect of life.

The results are a shared life that powerfully supports members in following Christ and a channeling of time and resources into Christian outreach. People in places as distant from each other as Norwood and Asbury Park, in as different states of life as the Weyands and Patricia Brennan, can be knitted together and support one another in Christ's service.

CHAPTER TWENTY

Rochester Fellowship Covenant Church

by Kevin Perrotta

Anyone wondering what Rochester Fellowship Covenant Church is all about had the opportunity to satisfy his curiosity a little this spring when members of the church presented a couple of hours of entertainment for relatives, friends and acquaintances. I accepted Pastor Loren Siffring's invitation to join them for the evening.

I was curious not only to learn more about the church but also to see how they presented themselves. They are an unusual group. Loren, a silver-haired, soft-spoken man I met several years ago, is a physician who has left medical practice to lead the church. The hundred-member church has no building, and it follows a schedule that does not include a worship service every Sunday. It is also characterized by a network of close-knit relationships among the members. What would they say about themselves that would answer outsiders' questions?

The evening's presentation was largely a blend of

patriotic reflections and Christian folk music. A string ensemble playing familiar patriotic airs accompanied a slide show of American wilderness, rural and urban scenes. A narrator added his comments. America, in one sense, is no special nation, he said, because if it disobeys God He will judge it as He would any other nation, while others will prosper. But God has blessed America, this land of natural endowments, brave immigrants and flawed freedoms. Why? What destiny has He appointed for it?

The message seemed to be that the members of Rochester Fellowship, despite their investment of time and energy in building relationships with one another, have concerns that are familiar to any American—a concern for the nation's quality of life, for its government.

The Joys of Family

After the slide presentation the program turned to live entertainment. Community members sang songs they had written, played chamber music, danced. The evening ended with several numbers by a guitar-playing man and his wife who sang of the joys of family life while their four young children pantomimed with a remarkable lack of self-consciousness.

The family orientation distinguished the program from much other evangelistic and inspirational music of the same genre. The group seemed to be saying to their audience that a commitment to family—"contented fathers, contented mothers and contented children," as Loren Siffring put it—is at the heart of their church.

The blend of public and personal concerns, I reflected afterward, accurately represented what I knew of the Rochester church. The church's members share the concerns of many other Christians today about the moral condition of American society and its future (although not everyone would hold the same particular political views). And they share the distinctive marks of evangelical Protestantism with millions of other evangelicals—an emphasis on bringing men and women to a personal commitment to Christ, a high view of authority of the Bible, and so on. What is different about them, however, was suggested by the accent on family in their evening program. As a church they seek to have a family kind of relationship with one another; and they have structured their life together to support their growth as families.

A "home group" meeting on a Wednesday evening a couple of weeks later gave me a more detailed picture of the church's community life. The ten or so people who gathered in the home of Rick and Theresa Dalton opened their time together with prayer—quiet spontaneous prayers interspersed with short choruses drawn from passages from one end of Scripture to the other. Rick, a salesman for a dictating equipment company, led the conversation that followed.

After a couple of announcements and inquiring about arrangements to help one of the men in the group move the following week, Rick asked if anyone had anything to share. Sue, a young single woman, described the help some men in the church had given her getting her car fixed. Loren and Rick told the group about a daytime visit they had made to Sue's place of employment—a hospice for the dying where she is a nurse. "Everyone thinks very highly of Sue," the two men reported.

I learned afterward that Sue works on an odd schedule and lives outside Rochester. To help draw her into community life the Daltons have invited her to spend

Wednesday afternoons—her day off—visiting at their home.

The issue of abortion surfaced in the conversation as the group turned its attention to what Rick called "prayer focus"—items for everyone to be praying for regularly. Some members of the community are involved in an anti-abortion educational project. The mention of abortion led into a discussion of a bill regarding sex education pending in the state legislature.

After a coffee break, Rick presented reflections on the twelfth chapter of John's Gospel. He contrasted the ambiguous enthusiasm of the crowds waving palm branches with the deep loyalty of Mary, who anointed Jesus' feet with nard worth a year's wages: going along with the pressure of the crowd versus individual commitment. "Individual decision—that's what community is based on," he said.

Pastors, Friends and Plans

When everyone left I questioned Loren and Rick about the dynamics of the group. The two men have worked together since the early seventies when Rick and Theresa were living with another couple and were "involved over our heads" in a Christian coffee house ministry to street people, folks from the mental hospital, and so on. Rick began looking to Loren for guidance and support, and the two have developed a close friendship.

Rick takes some pastoral concern for Sue, and for three of the men in his home group, with whom he meets weekly one on one. Two of those men, in turn, take some responsibility for helping the two remaining men in the group get established in the Christian life. These pastoral relationships are designed to give people practical wisdom and encouragement. For the married men a key concern is their learning to carry out their family responsibilities and to balance their family commitments with employment and service outside the home.

This particular home group has been together for some time, and the policy is not to move people from one small group to another unless there is a serious reason. "Where there's a 'flow' in the relationships," Loren put it, "we don't change them around." Thus there is a kind of natural growth, as new people come to the community and are added to existing sets of relationships.

During the week members of the group have informal contact with one another and give one another practical help. The Wednesday evenings are used in various ways. Sometimes Rick teaches from the Bible; sometimes the group does something recreational. Rick discusses his plans with Loren. He also tries to involve the other men in responsibility for the group. One of them, for example, was responsible for sorting through prayer requests to compile a "prayer focus" list of reasonable length.

Rochester Fellowship's life is in sets of relationships such as those I saw at the Daltons' house. The structure of the church follows the lines of the relationships rather than lines of institutional authority—pastor, board of elders, administrative board, youth ministry, Sunday school and the rest. Linking families together, meeting in homes, the church is structured in a way that supports family life rather than competes with it.

The gradual development of Rochester Fellowship Covenant Church has been both radical and balanced. The element of radical commitment has been present from the beginning, as the community grew up around men like Loren and Rick who, in the late sixties and early seventies, were overcommitted to youth ministry, evangelism, church renewal and Bible teaching, following a personal experience of the power of the Holy Spirit. Naturally they have attracted men and women who also want to make a radical commitment to God.

This continuing emphasis on radical conversion was visible in a small group meeting for newcomers which I attended. Ron Michell, one of the men in Rick's home group, led the meeting one evening in his apartment. The 15 men and women were gathered for the twelfth and final session of a series in which they made their way through a workbook explaining God's plan of salvation and the personal implications of placing one's life wholly under God's authority. The format was a reading of Scripture verses with comments and discussion.

Concrete aspects of the community demonstrate the members' willingness to make radical changes in their lives. To give only one example, several of the families have moved into Rochester from nearby towns. One man I spoke with told me he had done so at considerable financial cost, because Rochester is a more expensive place for him to live.

Along with depth of commitment and willingness to change, however, there has been an organizing principle that has given the church balance. Radical change has been involved as people have come into the church and entered its network of relationships; once there, however, people have found close personal ties that have supported them in living as Christians. So growth has been both radical and organic.

Loren and Rick have pulled back from many activities in order to give more balanced attention to their own families and to shepherd the other members of the community. They have invested time and effort in personal pastoral relationships and teaching aimed at helping the people who have joined the community get their family lives in order and learn to relate to one another in terms of service, mutual honor and generosity.

The pastoral investment in fostering stable personal relationships and Christian character has not turned the community's attention inward. Personal evangelism, the evening presentation which I attended, the anti-abortion educational project, the continuing concern about a variety of local and national issues—all signal an outward-looking stance.

Get Relationships Right

The combination of a call to radical Christian commitment and an emphasis on building personal relationships—with other principles, which I have not tried to discuss here—has yielded a church in which the member's faith, affection, hospitality and mutual care are quickly apparent to an outsider.

When I attended the church's Sunday service, an every-other-week gathering held at a publicly owned hall in a Rochester park, these qualities were noticeable. People immediately greeted my family, found extra chairs for us and even brought us coffee (the worship service is informal enough that a cup of coffee is not out of place). After a period of spontaneous worship and singing, members had an opportunity to share personal events, which might strengthen others' faith; for example, a man told how he had been protected from serious injury in a factory accident.

There was no one sermon, but Rick Dalton and two other men spoke for about 15 minutes each. Rick delivered a practical exhortation to set relationships right. "If your brother has wronged you, and you decide to hold it in, and not talk to him, the Holy Spirit will not give you peace. He urges you to get it right. If you have been wrong, go to your brother humbly: 'My attitude was wrong. Will you forgive me?' Get it straight." At the end of his talk, Rick gave everyone a couple of minutes to take pencil and paper and write down the names of people they needed to talk with to resolve problems in their relationships.

The exhortation to put scriptural instruction about personal relationships into practice typifies in some way the life of Rochester Fellowship. The pastoral vision of its leaders is not to develop an organization that excels at providing certain services to meet certain needs, such as preaching, Bible study, evangelism, counseling or social action. Rather their intention is to build up a people who are committed to the Lord and one another, in "covenant loyalty" as they would say. Providing particular services for particular needs will grow out of this.

CHAPTER TWENTY-ONE

The Word of God

by Charles H. Green and Kevin Perrotta

Family, friends and others often respond with puzzlement to the announcement, "I'm going to join a covenant community." Most people have only a vague notion—if that—of life in a covenant community and almost no understanding why anyone would be part of one.

The news that a relative or friend is becoming a member of a covenant community such as The Word of God, in Ann Arbor, Michigan, creates no clear picture in most people's minds. Will the person live on a commune? Does everyone wear long robes and sandals and carry a sign saying, "Repent, The End Is Near?" Will he have to stop watching sports on television?

Just what is a covenant community? What is The Word of God, and how does it work?

Ordinary Station Wagons

"The community," as its 1,500 adult members refer to it, is not a commune. They do not all live together. They do not dump their money into a common pot. They do not eat only yogurt, wild oats and honey. They do not go to Sunday worship in horsedrawn carts or vote a solid Republican ticket.

The Word of God is a group of normal men and women who decided they want to live in a strong Christian environment with other men and women who are also working hard to live as New Testament Christians.

Some do live together, sharing everything, devoting themselves to full-time Christian service. Others own homes in ordinary suburbs, drive ordinary station wagons, work at ordinary jobs and raise ordinary children who get into ordinary trouble.

People come from every area of organized, and unorganized, religion. They include people whose religious upbringing was strong and powerful and who joined the community while maintaining their loyalty and ties with their churches. There are people whose feet never crossed a church threshhold until one of the Word of God outreaches touched them. They are Roman Catholics, Jewish believers, Protestants of all flavors and a few Orthodox.

They were not drawn into community living because they have a lot in common on the natural plane. Members of The Word of God really have something quite simple in common: their love for Jesus Christ and acceptance of Him as Lord and savior.

We Might As Well Try

The community started in 1967 as an outgrowth of prayer meetings in a walk-up apartment near the campus of the University of Michigan.

Four young men, friends at the University of Notre Dame, had put aside budding careers and launched out into campus ministry. Their evangelistic efforts at Michigan State University, in East Lansing, had met with unexpected success when they became involved in the first wave of the Catholic charismatic renewal in the spring of 1967. But they met opposition too, and the summer found them looking for another campus. The Catholic student chaplain at the University of Michigan, in Ann Arbor, welcomed their help, even when they stressed their involvement in the charismatic renewal—praying in tongues, prophesying and all. "We've tried everything else," the priest shrugged, "and nothing has worked. I suppose we might as well try this." So in September they moved to town.

They began to do some personal evangelism and spent considerable time praying together. They sensed that God would lead them in new ways, now that they were aware of a wider variety of workings of the Spirit. It seemed better to wait on Him than to launch grand programs.

While they looked for something new, they were not without a sense of direction. Their outlook had been affected by an evangelistic movement they had worked with called Cursillo (Spanish for "short course" in Christianity). "We wanted to create a strong Christian environment, to find out what it really meant to be Christians in a body," Jim Cavnar, one of the original four men, recalls. "We were looking at the Scriptures to see how the early Christian communities worked."

Cavnar and the other three men—Steve Clark, Ralph Martin and Gerry Rauch—began a prayer meeting in their apartment on Thursday nights. The result was a kind of revival. College students and others came and encountered Christ powerfully and unexpectedly. People were introduced to prayer in tongues, prophecy and other gifts of the Spirit. In a few months the apartment was jammed on Thursday nights, and the meetings were moved to a church hall.

That You May Be Together

In the summer of 1969, the undefined group of campus ministry workers, college students and other young people began to hear a call from God that would shape their future.

The message, received largely through prophecy, was that God wanted to do more with them than turn individuals to Himself. "I brought you all here so that you may be *together*," they heard God say. "You cannot know and love Me perfectly unless you make yourselves a body. I am asking you to accept the covenant that I have given you."

"The idea for a covenant community came from that prophecy," Cavnar says. It was an unfamiliar idea, even a puzzling one. All Christians shared in the new covenant in Christ. How could there be an additional covenant? And what would commitment mean for the group of transient campus evangelists and college-age people? It took a summer of meetings and Scripture study, a weekend retreat and a year of struggle for understanding before the group felt that they had sufficiently grasped what "covenant" would mean for them.

The upshot of their reflections was that God wanted them to bind themselves to live out the new covenant in Christ as a particular body of Christians united with one another. A biblical model was seen in Josiah's action after the rediscovery of the book of the covenant in the temple. He and the people joined together in covenant to live out fully the covenant that God had already made with His people (2 Kings 23:1-3).

By fall 1970 this understanding had crystalized. At a second weekend conference, the 170 people came to a common mind on the basic principles involved in commitment to God and one another as members of a covenant community—what kind of personal commitment it would mean; how new people would be brought into the community; leadership. Each individual publicly assented to a formal one-page statement of the covenant.

Covenant and Commitment

"We opened our lives for God to use us and work with us as a body of people," Ralph Martin says. "When you read the covenant the thing that stands out is the relationship with God. It's nothing very complicated.

"We agreed on a *public* commitment to reinforce the covenant," Cavnar says. People embrace the covenant in two stages. After newcomers have been around for a while and have a chance to learn about community life, they are invited to make an "underway commitment" through which they agree to seek God with other community members during a training-evaluation stage. "The best way for a person to see if they are called to this commitment," Clark says, "is for them to live it out for a while."

Later they may be asked to make the "public commitment" in which they accept the full covenant by declaring in public that they want to give their lives fully to God and live as members of the community.

Both commitments are oral but both are serious

agreements made before God and community members. The public commitment is not necessarily lifelong, but release from it is undertaken only after serious prayer and counsel.

Martin singles out four practical areas of responsibility that members commit themselves to in the covenant: loving and serving one another, respecting community order, supporting the community financially, and taking part in community meetings and events. "These are merely ways of expressing the heart of the covenant, which is the agreement to live for God together."

In the summer of 1970 the community received another important prophecy, the one that gave the community its name, The Word of God. No one was more surprised by this prophetic word than the members of the community. As they have thought it over, they have come to believe that the community itself is a word from God to the churches about relatively neglected aspects of Christian life, such as the power of the Holy Spirit and the importance of Christians actually living as members of a body rather than as mere individuals.

Another "word" the community speaks is the possibility of Christians of different traditions sharing their lives with one another.

Cavnar and others in Ann Arbor believe that The Word of God was the first ecumenical covenant community in the United States. That ecumenical dimension makes The Word of God special, but it did not come about because of any great foresight by the founders. It just happened. The early prayer meetings attracted people from both Protestant and Catholic backgrounds. "When evangelism works, you'll get that," Martin says. "When the gospel spreads in the pluralistic

American situation, it spreads to neighbors, dormitory roommates, coworkers from various church backgrounds.

The group took this as an indication that God wanted a community made up of people who had—and maintained—different church loyalties. "It demonstrates that Catholics and Protestants can serve the Lord together," Martin says.

An Ecumenical Vision

Community life is based on the elements of Christianity that the various Christian traditions have in common. Community events do not involve teaching or practices that some members would not agree with because of their confessional stance.

But differences are recognized and respected, not ignored or passed over as unimportant. According to Cavnar, "We always felt strongly committed to our own churches, even though we were ecumenical from the very beginning."

The community saw a need to allow the different churches' teaching and sacramental life to be expressed within the community, without compromising the ecumenical character of activities that involve all the members. A solution was discovered in the creation of "fellowships" in 1980. These are local congregations composed mainly of members of The Word of God, guided by leaders of the community, and formally affiliated with church bodies in various confessional traditions.

Thus, many evangelical Protestant members of The Word of God belong to Emmaus Fellowship, a nondenominational congregation led by three evangelical community pastoral leaders. Many Lutherans belong to

Cross and Resurrection Lutheran Church, led by a Lutheran pastor who is a member of The Word of God. Many members from Reformed or Presbyterian backgrounds belong to Covenant Presbyterian Church, which is affiliated with the Evangelical Presbyterian Church. Christ the King functions as the parish for Roman Catholic members. It is guided by Catholic community leaders, and is pastored by two priests in the community under the oversight of Kenneth Povish, the local Catholic prelate, who played a major role in establishing the fellowship with the cooperation of other Catholic church officials. Some members of The Word of God do not belong to a community-sponsored fellowship but remain in area churches while joining in the full range of other activities in the community.

The four fellowships meet in separate locations on Sunday mornings. They offer doctrinal teaching for adults and children, perform baptisms, weddings, funerals, and provide for other aspects of church life that are not included in the community's activities.

Some people who join the community have never associated in depth with people from other churches. But defensiveness and prejudices fall quickly when people realize that no one is trying to attack their beliefs but that other members respect their convictions. As a result, members grow in appreciation of each other's church background.

The leaders of The Word of God have worked hard to maintain solid relationships with area clergy. Some local pastors are enthusiastic about the community. Most others are generally accepting of it, even if they do not agree entirely with everything about it.

There have been occasional difficulties over the years

as well. The enthusiastic style of worship favored by community members was disconcerting to some congregations. Some pastors feared that community members might be more loyal to the community than to their own denomination or church. These points of stress were alleviated by the formation of the fellowships, which enable members to integrate their existing church loyalties with their ties to The Word of God.

A Week in the Community

There is a definite pattern to life in The Word of God. Many Sunday afternoons there is a prayer meeting, with spontaneous praise, singing, use of spiritual gifts, sharing of experiences and teaching. These may be community-wide gatherings or they may be meetings of subunits of the community, called districts. Once a month the community sponsors a Family Forum for teaching and discussion about marriage and family life. Just as frequently, each district will gather for a social or recreation event.

Community members form small groups for prayer, Bible study and personal sharing one evening every week or two. Generally small groups of men and women meet separately.

Another evening may be taken up with one of several courses on living a committed Christian life. The courses are practical: how do I apply the teaching of Scripture to my life here and now? They range from ever-important basics such as growing in love for God or overcoming sinful habits, to aspects of Christian character and personal relationships, to sexuality, marriage and single life, to how to resolve disagreements within the community.

A group this size naturally has people of many talents,

and community entertainment evenings are a regular feature on the calendar. These range from musical concerts to theater to comedy to performances by visiting professionals sponsored by the community.

Community members visit each other's homes frequently. Saturday nights are reserved for a ceremony marking the start of the Lord's Day with a festive meal, often shared with others. Many families get together after Sunday church for brunch. Men's and women's groups set aside an evening once in a while for bowling or a baseball game or some other leisure activity.

Women in the community help each other with household tasks and meal preparation when there is a birth. Several men may pitch in to help a member of their small group paint his house. Some members open their homes for morning or evening prayer rooms. Some women have become experts at organizing the various details of a wedding and are greatly appreciated by brides who have much of that burden lifted from them.

All of this activity and mutual service, in Martin's words, "help us live better than we would without community. We keep each other inspired to follow Christ."

And that is the core of community life. Living in the midst of other Christians fosters a better relationship with God. When daily personal prayer is something everyone seeks, then it is easier to find your own personal prayer time. When you stumble in daily devotion or faithfulness to your responsibilities in life, there is someone close at hand to call you on.

"It is easier for me to follow the Lord because there are hundreds of others doing it with me," Martin says. "Without community it is much easier to let other goals slip into our lives. If I started to slip, someone would call me on. I appreciate that."

Who's in Charge Here?

Leadership of the community was entrusted to the original founders, who continue to serve, and to an expanding body of other leaders. As a group, the community elders, called coordinators, govern community life. Within the group some have overall responsibility while others care for the common life and pastoral needs of particular districts.

In the districts, which range from 100 to 200 people, other men and women work with the coordinators to provide personal pastoral care for all the members. These associate leaders include people at various levels of responsibility for the district and the small groups. Added together, a significant percentage of the members of the community are in some leadership role.

Coordinators come up through the ranks. Generally a man will begin leading a small group and doing other forms of service. As his experience grows and others see leadership qualities in him, he is given more responsibility, and additional training. Consultation with community members is built into the process, particularly at the point when a man begins to serve as coordinator on a temporary basis and again at the point, several years later, when he is made a more permanent member of the group of coordinators.

The coordinators are men, but women play key pastoral roles in the community. In each district, one or more women are formally designated to work with the coordinator to guide the pastoral care of women. Their role is modeled on the instruction of Titus 2:3-5 that the older women should "teach what is good, and so train the young women." They consult with him about women's experience of community life. They also teach, lead small groups, provide personal pastoral care and counseling to the women, and offer retreats.

Men and Women and Roles

The community encourages the expression of distinctive roles for men and women, seeing this as a way of capitalizing on the respective strengths of the sexes without undermining their fundamental equality.

All kinds of functions are open to women—evangelizing, teaching, decision-making, prophesying, charitable works. The community believes that Scripture and Christian tradition indicate that overall leadership in the Christian community and the family is given to men. But women also exercise leadership in pastoral care for women and in many community activities and outreaches.

"In the early 1970s, when we were in a very formative stage, feminism was becoming a strong influence," says Peter Williamson, a coordinator of the community and president of the Center for Pastoral Renewal. "We decided, nonetheless, to follow the New Testament teaching of male eldership. This was a hurdle for some folks to cross, but we felt we should hold fast to that principle and we're glad we have."

In the community's view, equality does not mean that men and women should be treated identically, but that the role of women should be as highly regarded as the role of men, and vice versa.

For instance, the role of women in the family and in the raising of children is accorded great honor in The Word of God. "We think it's discriminatory against women to put a lower value on the women's role in the family—a role in which men cannot replace them—than on women's roles as employees or administrators or professionals outside the home,'' Martin says.

Local and Global Mission

The impact of The Word of God goes far beyond the sense of brotherhood and sisterhood it gives the members. The impact comes from some specific community-sponsored outreach programs and from the efforts of individuals within The Word of God turning their hands to good works.

Teams of community members have assisted other groups of Christians around the world to form covenant community. In 1982 some of these other communities joined The Word of God to form one international, interconfessional community called The Sword of the Spirit. Since then, The Word of God has continued simply as a local branch of The Sword of the Spirit, which has branches and affiliates in more than 15 nations.

University Christian Outreach, a program of the whole Sword of the Spirit aimed at university students, is based in Ann Arbor. Most of the younger members of The Word of God found the Lord through the efforts of UCO. The organization touches thousands of college students groping for more meaning in their lives. The Sword of the Spirit's publishing outreach is also centered in Ann Arbor and is largely staffed by members of The Word of God. Under the umbrella of Servant Ministries the community has put books, music, and teaching tapes in the hands of hundreds of thousands of people. The Center for Pastoral Renewal, a division of Servant, has published *Pastoral Renewal* since 1976.

The Word of God sponsors breakfast and luncheon meetings with prayer and personal testimony directed at Ann Arbor area residents. Community members formed the Michigan Christian Association, an evangelistic organization that conducts series of meetings designed to bring people into a deeper relationship with Jesus. The series, called "A New Way of Living," is based on the "Life in the Spirit Seminars" that The Word of God developed in the early 1970s and that have played an important role in introducing people around the world to the charismatic renewal. Some people who participate in A New Way of Living feel called to membership in The Word of God. Many of the rest develop continuing friendships with members of the community while remaining as members of MCA.

Some of The Word of God's penetration of the general Ann Arbor community comes simply through individual members' daily work and witness in their jobs and neighborhoods. On their own initiative, members have set out to serve the people around them. A physician in The Word of God started a free clinic. A technical writer and his wife launched a crisis pregnancy counseling center. Some community members are foster parents. Many are active in school and community organizations. Some members are involved in politics; a few have run for political office.

Growing Pains

The Word of God is a continuously developing body of believers. At the beginning of the 1980s, a major step forward was inaugurated with a special training course for community members. The goal was to communicate an understanding of developments in secular society that challenge Christian living and to call members to a higher level of zeal in building a Christian culture on distinctively scriptural grounds. Small groups were to become more stable in membership, to provide greater personal support. Families would try to buy or build homes closer to others in their small groups in order to share their lives more deeply. The idea was to solidify members' lives so that more energy could be focused on mission and outreach.

The training course bore good fruit, but not without some pain. In retrospect the coordinators decided they had tried to do too much too quickly, causing tensions. Last year the coordinators made a report to the community in which they noted progress but asked forgiveness for failing to sufficiently monitor and pastor the process of change initiated by the training course.

Another long-range change in community life has resulted simply from the gradual aging of the first generation of college-age members and the addition of new members in their forties, fifties and older. What started as a community of young people has become predominantly a community of families. Intense community life-styles that worked well for singles and young people caused problems for families.

"We go through a process of making mistakes and correcting them," Williamson says. "Sometimes we get it right. Now we have about 1,000 children under the age of 13. We need to go a little higher up the mountain and reorient community life so that it is more hospitable to family life. We started as a community of singles. Now we are looking at developing family life in a way we never have before."

Part of the shift of emphasis included the foundation in 1981 of a community school for grades four through nine. After graduating, the children go on to local public or Christian schools.

The community has undergone another change as a

new wave of the Holy Spirit has spread through it in the last year. "We've always been characterized by use of spiritual gifts, charismatic style of worship, and so on," Martin says. "Lately, contact with other Christians, including John Wimber, has brought renewed emphasis on spiritual power."

The Word of God sponsors a "ministries clinic" two nights a month where community members and people from outside the community learn to pray for healing, to be guided by the Spirit in evangelism and to exercise other spiritual gifts. Prayer for healing is becoming an integral part of community meetings. There have been major physical and emotional healings as a result.

Members see this renewed experience of spiritual power as a sign of God's continuing initiative in the life of the community. Since the late 1960s, when campus evangelism yielded its first spate of profound conversions and the ill-defined group heard God's call to commitment in community, their ideal has been to see where God is at work and to work with Him. Members are quick to acknowledge that The Word of God has been God's idea from the beginning. They recognize that wisdom gained in the years of community life is useful only as everyone stays alert to the movement of the Spirit. Thus as The Word of God nears the 20-year mark, the community is thankful for what God has graciously done and is confident of His continued leadership in the future.

CONTRIBUTORS

John C. Blattner is executive director of the Center for Pastoral Renewal and editor of its monthly journal, *Pastoral Renewal*. He is an elder of The Word of God branch of The Sword of the Spirit, in Ann Arbor, Michigan, and author of *Growing in the Fruit of the Spirit* and *Death in the Nursery: The Secret Crime of Infanticide* (with James Manney).

Stephen B. Clark is president of the assembly of The Sword of the Spirit. His books include *Man and Woman in Christ*, *Unordained Elders and Renewal Communities* and *Building Christian Communities*.

Charles H. Green, a former correspondent for the Associated Press, teaches journalism at Michigan State University in East Lansing, Michigan.

Mike Guenther is an attorney and serves as an elder of The Word of God branch of The Sword of the Spirit in Ann Arbor, Michigan.

John Keating is international director of University Christian Outreach, an evangelistic and leadership development ministry to college students.

Ralph C. Martin is presiding elder of The Word of God branch of The Sword of the Spirit in Ann Arbor, Michigan. A prominent conference and television speaker, he is on the team of FIRE, a Catholic association for Faith, Intercession, Repentance and

Evangelism. He is the author of *A Crisis of Truth*; *The Return of the Lord*; *Husbands, Wives, Parents, Children*; and other books.

Kevin Perrotta is associate director of the Center for Pastoral Renewal, managing editor of its monthly journal, *Pastoral Renewal*, and director of its conference series, *Allies for Faith and Renewal*. He is the author of *Taming the TV Habit*.

Kevin Springer is a contributing editor to *Pastoral Renewal* journal and the editor of *Commonlife*, a quarterly journal concerning Christian community and renewal. Formerly the pastor of Servants of Christ community church in Port Huron, Michigan, he now works as a free-lance writer in Yorba Linda, California. He is co-author, with John Wimber, of *Power Evangelism*.

Suzanne Springer is the editor of *The Vineyard Newsletter*, a newsletter for members of Vineyard Christian Fellowships around the United States. She formerly served as a pastoral leader in Servants of Christ community church, in Port Huron, Michigan.

Peter S. Williamson is president of the Center for Pastoral Renewal and a senior elder in The Word of God branch of The Sword of the Spirit in Ann Arbor, Michigan.

Bruce Yocum is a senior elder of The Sword of the Spirit and oversees the development of new branch communities in Europe, Great Britain, Africa and the Middle East.

A Word About *Pastoral Renewal*

The same kind of analysis, insight and practical wisdom that characterize this book is available on a monthly basis in the pages of *Pastoral Renewal*.

Pastoral Renewal is a journal serving clergy and lay leaders in the Protestant, Catholic and Orthodox churches. It seeks to foster renewal in their vision for pastoral care and in the principles and methods of carrying it out. *Pastoral Renewal* offers practical advice, encouragement and wisdom for leaders' own lives, in a spirit of confidence in God's presence with, and action through, the leaders of His people.

To receive three months' worth of *Pastoral Renewal* on a trial basis, send your name and address to:

Pastoral Renewal
Dept. W
P.O. Box 8617
Ann Arbor, MI 48107

OTHER PUBLICATIONS OF INTEREST FROM CREATION HOUSE

The Emerging Christian Woman
by Anne Gimenez

Women are on the move. They are shaking off many years of unbiblical silence and passivity. Inspired by the Spirit, they are assuming their proper roles of leadership in the body of Christ. Anne believes Christ is calling Christian women to take a lead in bringing new life, healing and unity to the church. $4.95

Spiritual Power and Church Growth
by C. Peter Wagner

Why do some churches grow like wildfire? How can we learn from this marvelously successful church growth movement? C. Peter Wagner identifies the main reasons for the expansion of Pentecostal churches and articulates key principles behind their growth in Latin America. With examples, stories and facts, he writes about how to engage the power of the Holy Spirit; involving new Christians in ministry; cell groups; training leaders in service; the importance of signs and wonders; and other valuable principles. $6.95

Available at your Christian bookstore or from:

190 N. Westmonte Drive
Altamonte Springs, FL 32714